Based on a corpus of Texan oral narratives collected by the author over the past fifteen years, this study presents an analysis of the literary qualities of orally performed verbal art, focusing on the significance of its social context. Although the tales included are all from Texas, they are representative of oral storytelling traditions in other parts of the United States, including tall tales, hunting stories, local character anecdotes, accounts of practical jokes, and so on. They are also highly entertaining in their own right.

Professor Bauman's main emphasis is on the act of storytelling, not just the text. His central analytical concern is to demonstrate the interrelationships that exist between the events recounted in the narratives (narrated events), the narrative texts, and the situations in which the narratives are told (narrative events). He identifies these interrelationships by combining a close formal analysis of the texts with an ethnographic examination of the way in which their telling is accomplished, paying particular attention to the links between form and function. He also illuminates other more general concerns in the study of oral narrative, such as stability and variation in the oral text, the problem of genre, and the rhetorical efficacy of literary forms.

As an important contribution to the theoretical and practical literary analysis of orally performed narratives, the book will appeal to students and teachers of folklore, sociolinguistics and linguistic anthropology, and literary theory.

Cambridge Studies in Oral and Literate Culture   10

STORY, PERFORMANCE, AND EVENT

Cambridge Studies in Oral and Literate Culture

Edited by PETER BURKE and RUTH FINNEGAN

This series is designed to address the question of the significance of literacy in human societies: It will assess its importance for political, economic, social, and cultural development and will examine how what we take to be the common functions of writing are carried out in oral cultures.

The series will be interdisciplinary, but with particular emphasis on social anthropology and social history, and will encourage cross-fertilization between these disciplines: It will also be of interest to readers in allied fields, such as sociology, folklore, and literature. Although it will include some monographs, the focus of the series will be on theoretical and comparative aspects rather than detailed description, and the books will be presented in a form accessible to nonspecialist readers interested in the general subject of literacy and orality.

Books in the series

STORY, PERFORMANCE, AND EVENT

Contextual studies of oral narrative

RICHARD BAUMAN

Indiana University
Bloomington, Indiana

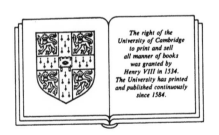

The right of the
University of Cambridge
to print and sell
all manner of books
was granted by
Henry VIII in 1534.
The University has printed
and published continuously
since 1584.

CAMBRIDGE UNIVERSITY PRESS

CAMBRIDGE

NEW YORK   NEW ROCHELLE

MELBOURNE   SYDNEY

Published by the Press Syndicate of the University of Cambridge
The Pitt Building, Trumpington Street, Cambridge CB2 1RP
32 East 57th Street, New York, NY 10022, USA
10 Stamford Road, Oakleigh, Melbourne 3166, Australia

First published 1986
Reprinted 1988

Library of Congress Cataloging in Publication Data
Bauman, Richard.
Story, performance, and event.
(Cambridge studies in oral and literate culture ;
10)
Bibliography: p.
Includes index.
1. Oral tradition.   2. Folklore – Performance.
3. Story telling.   I. Title.   II. Series.
GR72.B38   1986   398   85–29099

British Library Cataloging in Publication Data
Bauman, Richard
Story, performance and event : contextual
studies of oral narrative. – (Cambridge studies in
oral and literate culture; 10)
1.   Storytelling
I.   Title
808.5'43   LB1042

ISBN 0 521 32223 5 hard covers
ISBN 0 521 31111 X paperback

Transferred to digital printing 1999

CONTENTS

ACKNOWLEDGMENTS

There is a story about a traveler spending the night in a small West Texas town who joined a group of men sitting on the porch of the general store. After several vain attempts to start a conversation, he asked, "Is there a law against talking in this town?"

"No law against it," said one old-timer. "We just like to make sure it's an improvement on silence."

My last book was largely about silence. This one has more to do with the kind of talk done by men at the general store and with stories like this one. Whether it is an improvement on silence will be for readers to decide, but I do want to thank the individuals and institutions that helped endow it with such good qualities as it may have.

My greatest debt is to the storytellers whose verbal artistry provided the substance of this book. I regret that I can only thank Ed Bell by name, but I am no less grateful to those who have preferred to remain anonymous; I have employed pseudonyms to protect their privacy, and I offer them my sincerest thanks. I am grateful as well to Tom Green, Donna West, Pat Mullen, Pat Jasper, and Beverly Stoeltje for generously sharing their field data with me to supplement my own. Their collegial support made the book possible, and I am greatly in their debt. Inez and Roger Smith and Alma and Ed Bell have made me more than welcome during various stints of fieldwork, and I will always cherish their kind and willing hospitality. I have learned a great deal from them all.

A number of individuals have offered critical comments on portions of this book, which has benefited greatly from their insights: Keith Basso, Susan Gal, Erving Goffman, Tom Green, Michael Herzfeld, Pat Mullen, Frank Proschan, Beverly Stoeltje, and Greg Urban. I owe a special debt of gratitude to Roger Abrahams, Barbara Babcock, Dan Ben-Amos, Ruth Finnegan, and Joel Sherzer, who kindly read and commented on the entire manuscript; I am honored by their interest and their efforts on my behalf. Thanks too to Debora Kodish and Richard Hulan for bibliographical assistance and to Pat Jasper for aid with transcription.

The University Research Institute of the University of Texas at Austin provided funds that allowed me a semester off from other duties to write the first draft of this book. I am pleased to acknowledge this support.

Frances Terry, as always, has been an unstinting source of aid and energy through all the writing and rewriting, typing and retyping that finally produced the finished work. I thank her yet again for her skill, patience, and good humor.

I have already thanked Beverly Stoeltje as colleague, but that is not nearly enough. She has patiently inducted me into the mysteries of Texas culture, served as source and springboard for ideas, kept me as honest as she could as I tried to make sense of it all, and shared in the creative process all along the way. This book is for her.

NOTE ON THE TEXTS

This is far from an oral narrative collection in the traditional sense, but the reader will find something in the neighborhood of thirty primary texts presented in its pages. In recent years, the problematics of rendering oral texts in print have become the focus of much theoretical and methodological attention (see especially Fine 1984; Hymes 1981; Ochs 1979; Sherzer 1982a; Tedlock 1983), to the point where it is incumbent upon anyone who publishes oral texts to be explicit about the presentational format employed.

Discussions of this problem in intersemiotic translation center around the formal patterning principles that organize forms of oral discourse; the goal is to render the printed texts in such a way as to reveal the essential formal features of the texts presented, a kind of graphological laying bare of the device. What makes the task so problematic is that orally performed narrative, for example, will be organized by a complex and interpenetrating range of discourse and performance structures. One is thus confronted by the prospect of loading down the printed text with so much formal furniture that it is inaccessible to the reader, or alternatively of making motivated choices among presentational formats to emphasize specific patterning principles.

For my own part, I have been guided by pragmatic and problem-oriented considerations in the preparation of my texts. The textual materials are rendered in a number of different ways, variously highlighting rhetorical structures, interactional structures, narrative episodes, prosodic patterns, parallelism, and the like, depending on the analytical purpose at hand and with special attention to form–function interrelationships. At times, I have presented the same materials in more than one way, to bring out different points (cf. Woodbury 1985). The essential point is that every text I have presented reflects conscious attention to form on my part.

Beyond the matter of discourse and performance structures, one faces additional problems, partly analytical, partly ethical, in rendering spoken language in written form. For folklorists, many of the difficulties stem from the fact that the people to whom their attention is drawn tend to be speakers of nonstandard vernacular dialects that contrast especially markedly with the academic standard written English of the scholars' published reports. Regardless of one's intentions, then, rendering spoken vernacular language in print can convey an ill-defined mass of social information, rooted in stereotype and attitudes of inequality, which may be taken to reflect negatively on the people whose speech is being represented (Preston 1982).

Let me be explicit on two counts – the technical and the attitudinal – with regard to the language of these texts. My representation of spoken language is, frankly, intended to have more expressive than linguistic accuracy in a strictly technical sense. I am more interested here in the narratives as oral literature than as dialectological data. No words have been added or deleted (ellipses indicate hesitations or pauses),[1] no grammatical constructions "corrected," and no eye-dialect introduced, but I have attempted to convey that this is a record of language in a spoken, not a written, mode and to preserve something of the quality (however vague and impressionistic that term may be) of the oral discourse. To this end, I have selectively employed a variety of devices, some in themselves conventions for representing oral speech in print (e.g., "gonna," " 'bout") and some attempts to capture features of local pronunciation as employed by the speakers (e.g., "sumbitch," "hunnerd"). I have avoided, however, certain renderings of pronunciation that tend to evoke most readily features of negative stereotype, most notably "d-" for "th-" as in "dis" and "dat." A double slash (//) has been used to indicate simultaneity or overlapping of speech (i.e., when several people are talking at once). Above all, I would emphasize that no pejorative connotation of any kind is intended by the mode of presentation I have employed. My entire concern is to help illuminate and celebrate oral narrative for the artful accomplishment that it is.

---

[1]   When a previously introduced text is later excerpted, *bracketed* ellipses [. . .] are used to indicate omissions.

1

INTRODUCTION

Story, performance, and event

Some years ago, in a wry mood, a prominent American folklorist described folklore as "a bastard field that anthropology begot upon English" (Coffin 1968:v). This cute image has a certain rhetorical zip to it, but it is slanderously misleading as intellectual history. In truth, modern folklore has a fully honorable heritage; the seminal figure was that great precursor of romantic nationalism, Johann Gottfried von Herder, in whose vision the oral literature of a people was both the highest and truest expression of its authentic national culture and the appropriate foundation of its national literature.[1] There is an element of accuracy in the description, however, insofar as it suggests that academic compartmentalization and the stress on disciplinary integrity it engenders have compromised the legitimacy of folklore in some quarters, impeding its own pursuit of disciplinary autonomy within the academy. Scholars in anthropology and literature departments have generally remained willing to accord oral literature some place – however limited – within their own disciplinary purviews, but subject always to current fashions of intellectual concern and respectability.

My own conviction is that much has been lost as the rise of academic differentiation and its concomitant division of intellectual labor have fragmented the unified vision of literature as cultural production that was folklore's birthright. Scholars in literature departments operate within a frame of reference dominated by the canons of elite, written, Western literary traditions and texts, which tends to restrict consideration of oral literature to a search for sources and analogues of more cultivated literature or to such forms as the prettified versions of traditional Child ballads rendered by such culti-

---

[1] The term "oral literature" has come under criticism recently in writings on orality and literacy, so I need to account for my use of it here and elsewhere in this book. The problem is etymological: "literature," according to the argument, implies something to be read, but orally performed verbal art is preeminently to be *heard*. My own position, like that of Finnegan (1977:16), is that etymology is not a strong basis on which to base linguistic prescriptions. A classically trained scholar like Ong, with no field experience in the study of oral performance, might have trouble with the term (Ong 1982:10–15), but its wide currency and the weight of the research done in its name lead me to retain it, at least for now. Perhaps "spoken art," suggested by Sebeok (Bascom 1955:246 n. 9; see also Berry 1961), or "oral art," suggested by Herskovits (1961), would be preferable, but these terms have never achieved currency in any of the disciplines where they might serve a useful purpose – folklore, anthropology, or linguistics.

1

vated poets as Sir Walter Scott. Anthropologists, for their part, consider oral literature either as raw materials for the linguistic study of unwritten languages or as expressions, reflections, or support mechanisms for cultures and social structures. The social and the vernacular are excluded from the one discipline, the poetic from the other.

Fortunately, there have remained exceptions to these tendencies – intellectual figures like Edward Sapir, Kenneth Burke, Mikhail Bakhtin, or Roman Jakobson, who have maintained an integrated vision of the social and the poetic in the study of oral literature. This book is offered in the spirit of that integrative tradition.

The investigations on which this book is based were motivated by my long-standing interest in the ethnography of oral performance. The ethnographic perspective that has guided my work centers around a basic reorientation from a conception of folklore as things – texts, items, mentifacts – to verbal art as a way of speaking, a mode of verbal communication.

From the first emergence of the modern concept of folklore in the late eighteenth century until very recently, oral literature has been conceived of as stuff – collectively shaped, traditional stuff that could wander around the map, fill up collections and archives, reflect culture, and so on. Approached from this perspective, oral literature appears to have a life of its own, subject only to impersonal, superorganic processes and laws. But this view is an abstraction, founded on memories or recordings of songs as sung, tales as told, spells as chanted. We must recognize that the symbolic forms we call folklore have their primary existence in the action of people and their roots in social and cultural life. The texts we are accustomed to viewing as the raw materials of oral literature are merely the thin and partial record of deeply situated human behavior. My concern has been to go beyond a conception of oral literature as disembodied superorganic stuff and to view it contextually and ethnographically, in order to discover the individual, social, and cultural factors that give it shape and meaning in the conduct of social life.

My subject matter in this book is oral storytelling. Oral narrative provides an especially rich focus for the investigation of the relationship between oral literature and social life because part of the special nature of narrative is to be doubly anchored in human events. That is, narratives are keyed both to the events in which they are told and to the events that they recount, toward narrative events and narrated events (Jakobson 1971).

The radical interdependence of narrated events and narrative events is no new discovery. Walter Benjamin stated it well:

> The storyteller takes what he tells from experience – his own or that reported by others. And he in turn makes it the experience of those who are listening to his tale. (Benjamin 1969:87)

The problem, though, is how we are to attain a full understanding of this process. What we need is an analytical framework that can serve usefully and coherently for empirical investigations of the relationships among the elements, and this brings us up against well-entrenched divisions of intellectual labor. The indivisible work has indeed been divided in traditional scholarly practice. Literary theorists occasionally look outward from the texts toward the relationship between narratives and the events they recount, whereas anthropologists tend to look in the other direction, toward the relationship between narratives and the events in which they are performed.

I have myself been engaged for some years in the formulation of a performance-centered conception of oral literature, with primary attention to the performance event (Bauman 1977a,b, 1983; Paredes and Bauman 1972). Briefly stated, I understand performance as a mode of communication, a way of speaking, the essence of which resides in the assumption of responsibility to an audience for a display of communicative skill, highlighting the way in which communication is carried out, above and beyond its referential content. From the point of view of the audience, the act of expression on the part of the performer is thus laid open to evaluation for the way it is done, for the relative skill and effectiveness of the performer's display. It is also offered for the enhancement of experience, through the present appreciation of the intrinsic qualities of the act of expression itself. Performance thus calls forth special attention to and heightened awareness of both the act of expression and the performer. Viewed in these terms, performance may be understood as the enactment of the poetic function, the essence of spoken artistry. Accordingly, performance may be dominant in the hierarchy of multiple functions served by speech, as in what Dell Hymes (1974:444) has called ''full performance,'' or it may be subordinate to other functions – referential, rhetorical, or any other.

Oral performance, like all human activity, is situated, its form, meaning, and functions rooted in culturally defined scenes or events – bounded segments of the flow of behavior and experience that constitute meaningful contexts for action, interpretation, and evaluation. In the ethnography of oral performance, the performance event has assumed a place beside the text as a fundamental unit of description and analysis, providing the most concretely empirical framework for the comprehension of oral literature as social action by directing attention to the actual conduct of artistic verbal performance in social life (see, e.g., Abrahams 1982; Ben-Amos 1975; Briggs 1985; Duranti 1980; Falassi 1980; Finnegan 1977:153–60; Georges 1969).

The first task in the study of performance events is to identify the events themselves in ways consistent with local understandings and relevant to the analytical problems at hand. Events may be locally defined in terms of setting (e.g., Bauman 1972a), institutional context (e.g., Bloch 1975; Brenneis 1978), scheduling or occasioning principles (e.g., Abrahams 1977), and so on. The structure of performance events is a product of the systemic interplay of numerous situational factors, prominently including the following:

1. Participants' identities and roles (e.g., Bauman 1972b; Stoeltje 1981:136–9)
2. The expressive means employed in performance (e.g., Cosentino 1982:88–143)
3. Social interactional ground rules, norms, and strategies for performance and criteria for its interpretation and evaluation (e.g., Burns 1983:19–24; Darnell 1974)
4. The sequence of actions that make up the scenario of the event (e.g., Falassi 1980)

I have treated these matters in an earlier work (Bauman 1977b) in much fuller detail than this brief introduction will permit, but the guiding effect of the general perspective should become clear throughout the pages that follow.

As with every aspect of culture, the conventionalized, patterned organization of performance events is amenable to generalized ethnographic description. The ethnographic construction of the structured, conventionalized performance event standardizes and homogenizes description, but all performances are not the same, and one wants to be able to comprehend and appreciate the individuality of each as well as the general structures common to all. Every performance will have a unique and emergent aspect, depending on the distinctive circumstances at play within it. Events in these terms are not frozen, predetermined molds for performance but are themselves situated social accomplishments in which structures and conventions may provide precedents and guidelines for the range of alternatives possible, but the possibility of alternatives, the competencies and goals of the participants, and the emergent unfolding of the event make for variability (cf. Firth 1961:40).

As with event structures, so too with texts and social relations. The models provided by generic conventions and prior renditions of "traditional" items stand available to participants as a set of conventional expectations and associations, but these may themselves be used as resources for creative manipulation, shaping the emergent text to the unique circumstances at hand. The normative social structure and interaction order may provide similarly constituted expectations, but performance, like any form of communication, carries the potential to rearrange the structure of social relations within the performance event and perhaps beyond it (see, e.g., Limón 1983). The structure of social roles, relations, and interactions; the oral literary text and its meaning; and the structure of the event itself are all emergent in performance. The collective, the communal, the conventional are not forsaken here (contra Fowler 1981:190): rather, the individual and the creative are brought up to parity with tradition in a dialectic played out within the context of situated action, a kind of praxis.

But what of narrated events, the other anchor point of "the work in the totality of all its events" (Bakhtin 1981:255)? Current literary interest in narrated events and their relationship to narrative centers around two principal issues: the formal relationship between narratives and the events they recount, and the ontological and epistemological status of the narrated events themselves.

The first issue can be – and nowadays frequently is – framed as a problem of iconicity (e.g., see Enkvist 1981; McDowell 1982; Scholes 1981). Events are action structures, organized by relationships of causality, temporality, and other such linkages; narratives are verbal structures, organized by rules of discourse. Most commonly, narratives are seen as verbal icons of the events they recount, and the problem is one of determining the nature and extent of the isomorphism between them and the means by which this formal relationship is narratively achieved.

Although one may still find rather simple formulations of the formal correspondences between narratives and narrated events, the predominant thrust of modern narrative theory since at least the Russian formalists has been directed toward exploration of the formal literary devices that operate upon "external events" such that the rendering of those events in narrative discourse transforms them into simultaneously structurally different and structurally related constructions (e.g., see Chatman 1978; Genette 1980; Rimmon-Kenan 1983). Thus, for example, temporal structures may be displaced (as in flashback, or beginning in medias res), the point of view and voice through which the event is reported may be managed in ways impossible in the "real" world (the narrative may be presented through the voice of an omniscient observer, or the eyes of a horse), and so on.

The second problem, as noted, has to do with the nature and apprehension of the narrated event itself. There has been a widespread tendency to view narratives as icons of events, that is, to consider events as somehow antecedent or logically prior to the narratives that recount them, even, interestingly, in the case of fictional narratives, about events that never "actually occurred." The narratives are the signs, the events their external referents.

An alternative view, now beginning to attract more and more proponents, is that events are not the external raw materials out of which narratives are constructed, but rather the reverse: Events are abstractions from narrative. It is the structures of signification in narrative that give coherence to events in our understanding, that enable us to construct in the interdependent process of narration and interpretation a coherent set of interrelationships that we call an "event" (e.g., Mink 1978, 1981; Smith 1981). To this view, however, I would want to add – and to demonstrate in the studies that follow – that for all that "narrative is a primary cognitive instrument [for] making the flux of experience comprehensible" as event (Mink 1978:131), it may also be an instrument for obscuring, hedging, confusing, exploring, or questioning what went on, that is, for keeping the coherence or comprehensibility of narrated events open to question. If we assume with Goffman (1974:8) that "when individuals attend to any current situation, they face the question: 'What is going on here?'," we can assume as well that in storytelling situations a second question is added to the first with regard to the situations being narrated: "What was going on there?" And just as the answer(s) to Goffman's basic framing question may be problematic, so too may the answer(s) to the second one – and intentionally so.

Leaving the issue of priority open for the present – for I will want to address it explicitly later, in Chapter 3 – the perspective I have just outlined, by focusing jointly on narration and interpretation, provides a productive basis for an integrated framework that comprehends narrated event and narrative event within a unified frame of reference. The narrated event, as one dimension of a story's meaning, evoked by formal verbal means in the narrative text, is in this respect emergent in performance, whatever the external status of the narrated event may be, whether it in some sense "actually occurred" or is narratively constructed by participants out of cultural knowledge of how events are – or are not, or may be – constituted in social life. Thus, we can comprehend narrated event as well as narrative event within our overall concern with the interplay between the given available resources and patterns of narrative performance and the emergent functions and outcomes of that performance. This, then, in its broadest synthetic terms, sets the conceptual parameters of the chapters that make up this book.

Each of the individual chapters deals with a specific oral narrative tradition and is addressed to a particular analytical problem. The fieldwork on which these studies are based was conducted in Texas over the past fifteen years, but the expressive traditions I have dealt with are in fact quite widespread and familiar to all North American folklorists: tall tales, stories of coonhounds and dog traders, local anecdotes, and stories about practical jokes; fishing and hunting camps, trade days, family gatherings, and other sociable encounters. I have favored these classic genres and settings for several reasons, including such mundane ones as accessibility and personal taste, but most importantly for the strategic purpose of demonstrating that new perspectives do not necessarily demand the abandonment of old interests, as some seem to fear, but should lead to a reinvigoration of traditional concerns. At the same time, I am sensible that part of the price of this conservatism is a distinct bias toward male expressive traditions, which must be acknowledged in our pursuit of understanding of the role of gender in expressive culture.

As regards the analytical problems I have addressed, they represent a mix of the old and the new. Central to a number of the chapters, for example, is the classic problem of genre – the formal definition of narrative genres, the functional and transformational interrelationships that link them into larger expressive systems, and so on. The nature and role of expressive lying – from dog stories, to tall tales, to practical jokes – represents a second common thread that runs throughout these pages. And that most fundamental of folk-loric – indeed, cultural – problems, the dynamics of stability and change in symbolic forms, is analyzed in formal terms in Chapter 4 and in both formal and contextual terms in Chapter 5. At the same time, I have taken up a number of issues less commonly addressed by folklorists. In Chapter 2, on dog trading, for instance, I explore the strategic uses of narrative in social interaction. Chapter 3, on stories about practical jokes, analyzes the expressive construction of narrated events, followed in the next by an investigation of form–function interrelationships in local anecdotes. And Chapter 5 closes with a consideration of the implications of publicly oriented folklore programs for traditional performers.

My analytical strategy in tackling these problems is rooted in my systemic conception of oral narrative performance as the indissoluble unity of text, narrated event, and narrative event. Any component of performance may serve as a point of entry into the system, the nexus of the interrelationships to be explored, as suggested by the data themselves and the analytical question at hand, but it is the interrelationships that are crucial. A given chapter may foreground the text, the narrative event, or the narrated event, but no chapter ignores any one of them or the connections that bind them together.

I opened this introduction with a polemic against the severing of the social from the poetic, the anthropological from the literary, in the study of oral literature, and have devoted the rest of it to outlining the guiding principles by which my studies of oral narrative endeavor to narrow the gap. Now, at the end, I want to situate what I have attempted in this book within a broader intellectual context.

One may identify two lines of inquiry in current empirical explorations of oral literary forms in relation to written literature. The first of these, with which I associate my own work, is centrally concerned with understanding oral literature *as* literature, that is, as verbal art. This enterprise sets itself against some old and deeply entrenched concepts of the nature and qualities of oral literature. These notions, strongly colored by ethnocentric and elitist biases that privilege the classics of Western written literature over oral and vernacular literature and by nineteenth-century conceptions of "folk" society, have established an image of oral literature as simple, formless, lacking in artistic quality and complexity, the collective expression of unsophisticated peasants and primitives constrained by tradition and the weight of social norms against individual creativity of expression. This is no straw man, constructed to rationalize my own agenda; numerous recent works survey the legacy of these powerful biases as a point of departure for attempting to overturn them (e.g., Bauman 1982; Crowley 1966:1–7; Dundes 1964:15–29; Finnegan 1977).

These revisionist attempts have been concentrated on several fronts. One strong set of efforts has been devoted to discovering and elucidating the essential artfulness of oral literature, finding elegance of form in the "formless" and complexity in the "primitive." These discoveries rest on close formal analysis of the poetic devices that organize oral literary forms and performances: narrative structures (e.g., Dundes 1964), patterns of measured verse and other mechanisms of line and discourse structuring (e.g., Basso 1985; Hymes 1981; Sherzer 1982a; Tedlock 1983; Woodbury 1985), formal means of establishing verisimilitude (e.g., Tedlock 1983:159–77), manipulation of narrative time (e.g., Basso 1985:29–31; Nicolaisen 1982; Stewart 1982), metanarration (e.g., Babcock 1977), parallelism (e.g., Fox 1977), and so on. Still in its relative infancy, this movement has already brought us to an unprecedented level of understanding of the poetics of oral literature.

Closely related to these ethnopoetic investigations (if I may appropriate and generalize the term) – indeed, an integral part of the ethnopoetic enterprise – has been the burgeoning of the performance-centered perspective, founded on the realization that the essence of oral literature, including its artfulness, is not to be discovered in folklore texts as conventionally conceived, but in lived performances. In respect to form, for example, a performance orientation has led to discoveries of patterning principles realized in performance but obscured by older notions of verbal texts – features of prosody and paralanguage, of dialogic construction, of oral characterization. This, in turn, has led to a powerful reconceptualization of the nature of oral text and of the problematics of text making and translation in the presentation of oral texts in print (see Note on the texts preceding this Introduction). And the understanding of performance as fundamentally social has opened the way to the elucidation of form–function relationships of which we have hitherto had only impressionistic inklings at best.

A further notable consequence of our deeper awareness of the artfulness of oral literature and the radical importance of performance as constitutive of verbal art has been the restoration of the work of oral literature to the individual artist who produced it and a recognition of the creative individuality of the performer's accomplishment. When one views the item of folklore as the collective product and possession of society at large, the performer is reduced to the role of passive and anonymous mouthpiece or conduit for the collective tradition. The ethnography of performance, attuned to the unique and emergent aspects of performance as much as to the traditional, conventional ones, presents us with not merely a Bini story, but the impressive oral literary accomplishment represented by Aimiyekeagbon Ogbegbor's narrative of the Oba Ewuakpe (Ben-Amos 1977), not merely a Clackamas myth, but the stark and harrowing tragedy of "The Sun's Myth," by Charles Cultee (Hymes 1975), not merely a Texas tall tale, but the masterful performance by Ed Bell of "The Bee Tree" (Chapter 5). This point is that the student of oral literature, no less than the scholar of written literature, confronts individual folk poets and unique works of literary creation, worthy of critical attention as such, as artists and works of art.

This, then, has been the larger context of my work, the intellectual charter for this book. If I have been at all successful, the book will take its place first of all as a contribution to our expanding appreciation of oral literature as verbal art. There are, however, some still larger implications of these efforts that I would like to suggest, and this brings me to the second line of inquiry I mentioned earlier, namely, the investigation of orality and literacy in human culture.

Literacy has long been an important typological factor in anthropological thought, but we are currently in the midst of a strong resurgence of interest in the contrast between orality and literacy as two distinct expressive modes, marked by formal and functional differences (see, e.g., Goody 1977; Ong 1982; Opland 1983; Tannen 1982). Although it may at first appear that this concern to differentiate orality from literacy is at cross-purposes with ethnopoetic efforts to blur the boundaries between oral and written literature, the goals of the two fields are quite compatible. In fact, the lines of research are closely convergent at a number of key points: Albert Lord's seminal studies of oral epic (1960), for example, have been strongly influential in both areas, and there is a common ground of interest in the formal organization of oral discourse that unites the two. Ultimately, the pursuit of both sets of studies is directed toward a fuller understanding of the role of language in the conduct and constitution of social life.

The potential contribution of the ethnography of oral literature to the larger study of orality and literacy is quite clear. Not only do our investigations yield empirical information about *artful* uses of oral language – a dimension missing from most of the linguistically oriented explorations of the problem – but the ethnographic perspective demands that the verbal art forms of a society be comprehended as part of larger social and cultural systems organizing the social use of language. The more we can discover about oral literature within this broader frame of reference, the more we will know about oral uses of language in general. Already, the ethnography of oral literature has provided much-needed correctives to some of the more a priori and overgeneralized conclusions that have compromised some recent works in this field. Ruth Finnegan (1977) and Joel Sherzer (1982b), for instance, have provided ethnographic evidence controverting the insistence of Albert Lord (1960), Walter Ong (1982), and others that there cannot be verbatim memorization of fixed texts in oral cultures. Nor can one examine Victoria Howard's remarkable narrative, "Seal and Her Younger Brother Lived There," as explicated by Dell Hymes (1981:274–341), or Caswell Rogers's tightly structured and climactically concluded anecdotes, as analyzed later in this book, and sustain without strong qualification the argument, again made by Ong, that "an oral culture . . . cannot organize even shorter narrative in the studious, relentless climactic way that readers of literature for the past 200 years have learned more and more to expect'' (Ong 1982:143). To take a third example, an earlier version of my own essay on dog trading and storytelling (revised for this volume) led William Labov to qualify his assertion that ''A narrative that is judged entirely false, 'nothing but a big lie,' does not have the impact or acceptability of a narrative that is considered essentially true'' (Labov 1982:228, 245–6), by acknowledging the contrast between certain artful traditions of oral storytelling and the more simple, less practiced narratives of his own sources. The essential point is that if we are to free ourselves from orality versus literacy as a gross typological construct and make real progress toward an understanding of speaking and writing in human life, we must do so on the basis of soundly empirical, cross-cultural investigations. The ethnography of oral literature will play an important part in this endeavor, as it has from the beginning. The payoff will be great for all the human disciplines.

2

"ANY MAN WHO KEEPS MORE'N ONE HOUND'LL LIE TO YOU"

A contextual study of expressive lying

"There are two kinds of tales, one true and the other false," Socrates proposes to Adeimantos in the course of exploring the proper place of literature in *The Republic* (376e), and the truth value of narrative – one dimension of the relationship of stories to the events they recount – has been a basic typological criterion in the classification of narrative ever since. Folklorists, for their part, have relied rather heavily on the truth factor in classifying oral narrative forms. For some, the basic distinction rests on "the extent to which a narrative is or is not based upon objectively determinable facts" (Littleton 1965:21), whereas others are more pragmatic and relativistic, relying on local distinctions made by members of the societies in which the tales are told between "narratives regarded as fiction" and "narratives . . . regarded as true by the narrator and his audience" (Bascom 1965:4).

Recently, however, there have been increasing expressions of unease about the empirical basis and reliability of such truth-value criteria. Herbert Halpert, for example, reports frequent baffled disagreement between himself and his students in the application of the truth–fiction distinction to the sorting out of jests and anecdotes, local legends, tall tales, and personal narratives (1971:51). Robert Georges, in turn, sees the truth–fiction question as so empirically clouded in actual cases that "the only *meaningful* answer would have to be an ambivalent one" (1971:17, emphasis in the original). Arguing from a most revealing transcript of a storytelling event, Linda Dégh and Andrew Vázsonyi take a preliminary step toward formulating an empirical basis for investigating the problematics of the truth value and believability factors, at least with regard to legends. "Objective truth and the presence, quality, and quantity of subjective belief are irrelevant," they maintain (1976:119). What is important is that legend "takes a stand and calls for the expression of opinion on the question of truth and belief" (1971:119). As observed by José Limón, "In some instances 'belief' may be quite secondary to performance itself" (1983:207). That is, if one may extend the point, considerations of truth and belief will vary and be subject to negotiation within communities and storytelling situations. This would suggest that if we are interested in the place of narrative in social life, it is the dynamics of variability and negotiation that we should investigate; the issue should be transformed from a typological comparative one to an ethnographic one. Abstract, a priori, and universalistic truth-value criteria or classificatory systems for oral narrative based on them have revealed themselves to be no more empirically productive than such a priori etic schemes have proved to be in other cultural spheres. Still, evidence indicates that truth and lying may well be of social and cultural concern to members of communities with regard to stories. What is needed are closely focused ethnographic investigations of how truth and lying operate as locally salient storytelling criteria within specific institutional and situational contexts in particular societies (e.g., Heath 1983:149–89; Rickford 1986). That is what I have attempted here, in an exploration of storytelling and dog trading in Canton, Texas.

Canton is a small town of approximately 3,000 people, located about sixty miles east and a little south of Dallas. Its principal claim to fame is that on the Sunday preceding the first Monday of every month Canton becomes the scene of a large and very popular trading fair. The average attendance is about 20,000 – perhaps double that on Labor Day. The fair draws traders and dealers from as far away as New York, California, Oregon, and Minnesota.

First Monday at Canton – for so it is still called, although the action has shifted to Sunday in accommodation to the modern workweek – fits into a long tradition of American trade days. These seem to have originated in this country before the middle of the seventeenth century, in conjunction with the sitting of the county courts (Craven 1949:167). These courts met as often as once a month in some convenient spot, corresponding to the shire town of England or New England. Court day was a holiday, an occasion on which county residents came into town not only in connection with court functions, but to transact all kinds of business: to discuss public affairs, hold auctions, trade, and visit on the courthouse green (Carson 1965:195–6; Fiske 1904:62–6; Verhoeff 1911:7n). County courts usually met on the first Monday of the month – hence the term ''First Monday.'' Although the sitting of the court was the nucleus around which the court days first developed, the occasion became a social institution in its own right; Sydnor (1948:34) calls it one of the most important in the antebellum South. As political organization changed, however, and county courts developed other schedules, trade days often disengaged from court sessions to become autonomous occasions; they continued to be economically and socially important to the people of the regions in which they were held.

From the beginning, an important commodity in the trading that went on during First Mondays was horses and mules. Professional horse and mule traders were called ''jockies''; thus ''Jockey Day'' and ''Hoss Monday'' are other names for the occasion, and ''jockey ground'' or ''jockey yard'' designate the area in which the trading was conducted (Sartain 1932:253). Numerous local histories and personal documents testify to the high degree of interest and excitement generated by the action on the jockey ground during the height of the trade days in the nineteenth and early twentieth centuries.

But, as horses and mules declined in importance with the mechanization of Southern agriculture, First Monday trade days declined as well, to the point that very few now remain. Still, some trade days have been in continuous existence since they began, whereas others have been revived, reincarnated as flea markets.

First Monday in Canton, like most others, began in conjunction with a county court day; Canton is the county seat of Van Zandt County. The event developed in the years following the Civil War, probably during the early 1870s (Mills 1950:191–2). Like most others, too, this trade day became as much or more an occasion for coming to Canton as for attending to court business. Until 1965, the trading took place in the courthouse square, but by the mid-sixties the crowds simply got too big, and separate grounds were set aside. More than 1,000 lots are available on the trading ground, and more are being added all the time. The entire event is now sponsored by the Canton Chamber of Commerce.

Although an occasional mule or two is still hauled to Canton for trade and a considerable amount of domestic poultry is sold there as well, where animals are concerned, coon dogs are the real focus of interest during First Monday. This dog trading was an early feature of Canton First Monday. No one seems to know precisely when it began, but my oldest sources, who are past eighty years of age, remember it from their earliest visits to Canton. In 1960, a few years before the general trading left the courthouse square for separate grounds, the dog trading was moved to its own site across the highway from the main area, down on the river bottom. The dog grounds and dog trading are not part of the Chamber of Commerce operation. The grounds are privately owned, and the dog trading generally has a very different tone from the flea-market atmosphere across the road.

First, whereas many of the flea-market dealers and public are women, the people on the dog grounds are almost exclusively men. Again, the flea market attracts many urban types as well as townspeople from surrounding towns. On the dog grounds one sees mostly rural people – farmers, hunters, more blacks, and more people of lower socioeconomic status generally. The activity on the dog grounds begins in earnest on Friday night, when people begin to gather, set up tents and campers, stake out their dogs, drink, play cards, shoot dice, talk dogs, go off into the surrounding countryside to hunt, and generally have a good time.

At the peak of the trading, there are hundreds of hunting dogs of all kinds on the dog grounds, although coonhounds are clearly predominant. Some coon-dog men are as serious as other dog fanciers about breeding, standards, registration, papers, and the other trappings of "improving the breed." Most dealing in dogs at this level involves fancy stud fees, careful records, big money – into the thousands of dollars for a top dog. Many hound-dog men, however, are far more pragmatic. They just want good, working hunting dogs, and cannot afford to pay a great deal of money for them. These men tend to be less careful about the niceties of breeding, record keeping, and so on; they are satisfied with whichever dogs get together behind the shed, breeding "old Handy to old Ready." This is the group of dog traders that comes to Canton, and as a group they tend not to be highly regarded by the serious coon-dog breeders or by the townspeople in general. One citizen of Canton described dog traders to me as people for whom "making a living gets in the way." Some are professional dog jockies; most are amateurs. Their motivations for coming to Canton are various and often mixed. Some come to get "using dogs," whereas others just like to "move their dogs around" or "change faces." The professionals come to make some money, but many traders just want the activity to pay for itself – that is, to pay for the trip and for the dogs' feed.

The dominant reasons for coming to Canton, though, are to get together with other hound-dog men to talk about dogs and hunting, and to trade for its own sake, as recreation. For most traders at Canton, the economic motive is far from the top of the list; dog trading for them is a form of play, a contest of wits and words. Some men actually keep one or two dogs around at any given time just to trade and, not surprisingly, these are usually rather "sorry" dogs, "old trashy dogs that ain't worth a quarter for nothin'." One trader put it this way:

> My experience is, I'll be in Canton in the morning, be there Sunday all day, I've got a dog trade always. Reason I want to go because a man's gonna meet me there and demonstrate his dog and I'm gonna take mine. Course the one I'm gonna take ain't much of a dog. . . . Now and then I get a good dog, then I get one that ain't worth bring-in' home, but still it's trade that I like to do. (Recorded by Thomas A. Green, Blooming Grove, Texas, May 31, 1968)

In other words, Canton is "where the action is" (see Goffman 1967). Of course, no dog trader is averse to making some money, and one of the stated goals of any swap is to "draw boot" – that is, to get a dog and some cash for your dog. One man told me that his fellow traders would "trade with you for ten when ten's all they got in their dog, then they'll make five on your dog." These are small sums, though. In most cases, cash profit stands as a token of having played the game well; it is a sweetener that enhances the encounter. It is also true that many of the transactions at Canton are straight cash sales, but the dynamic of these transactions is the same in all essentials as trading, and they are considered to be and labeled trades.

When I asked what brought him to Canton, one old trader, who has been coming to First Monday for more than seventy years, replied, "Well, I enjoy trading and enjoy seeing my old friends." For him, as for most others on the dog grounds, the essence of First Monday is trading and sociability. I propose in the remainder of this chapter to explore some of the interrelationships between the two activities.

As a point of departure, let us consider the following two excerpts from dog-trading encounters at Canton. The first involves two participants: John Moore, a black man in his early forties, and Mr. Byers, a white man in his early fifties. John Moore has the dogs, and Byers has just walked up to look them over.

Byers:　He strike his own fox? [That is, can he pick up the fox's trail by himself?]

Moore:　He strike his own fox. Strike his own fox. Clean as a pin, strike his own fox. [Pause] And he'll stand to be hunted, he'll stand to be hunted [Byers interrupts – unintelligible]. What is that?

Byers:　He run with a pack good?

Moore:　Oh yes, oh yes. And he'll stand . . . he'll stand three nights out a week. He has did that and took off – ain't seen him waitin' behind that. [Unintelligible.] He'll stand three nights out a week. I've known that to happen to him. [Pause]

I try to be fair with a man 'bout a dog. Tell the truth about a dog, tell you what he'll do. If there's any fault to him, I wanna tell the man. If I get a dog from a man, if there's any fault to him, I want him to tell me.

I bought . . . we bought some puppies from a man, we asked him, said, "they been vaccinated?" Said, "now we gonna buy the puppies," say, "now if they been vaccinated, we wanta know if they ain't." Say, "now, what we's gettin' at, if they ain't been vaccinated distemper's all around." We wanted 'a vaccinate 'em.

And he swore they was vaccinated and after we bought 'em they died, took distemper and died. Then he told a friend o' ours, he say he hate that he didn't tell us that the dogs, the puppies, wasn't vaccinated.

See, and I begged him, "I tell you somethin' man, we gonna buy the puppies, gonna give you a price for 'em," I said, "but there's one thing we just wanta know if they been vaccinated." And then turned right around . . . then turned right around and told the man that they hadn't been vaccinated. And here I begged him, "I'm beggin' you, gonna buy the dogs, puppies, at your price."

Byers:　I traded two good coon dogs for two Walker dogs [a breed of hounds] –

Moore:　//Mmm hmm.

Byers:　//– supposed to be good fox dogs.

Moore:　Mmm hmm.

Byers:　Sumbitches wouldn't run a *rabbit*.

Moore:　You see that?

Byers: Boy, I mean they woundn't run nothin'.

Moore: I tell you for . . . what is your name?

Byers: Byers.

Moore: Mr. Byers, this here is John Moore, everybody know me here. I can take you to some people in here any day – I'm talkin' about some rich, up-to-date people – I have sold dogs to, and they'll tell you. . . . I'm talkin' 'bout for hunnerd dollars, some hunnerd dollar dogs, seventy-five dollar dogs, fifty dollar. . . . I haven't got a dog over there for fifty dollars. You can't raise one for that, 'cause a sack o' feed down there where we live cost you four fifty for fifty pounds, what we feed the hounds on, we feed the hounds on, and then we get scraps from that slaughter pen to put in. And if I tell you somep'n 'bout a dog I'm not gon' misrepresent him. Not gonna misrepresent him.

You see that little ol' ugly gyp [bitch] there? She'll git in the thicket. . . . We was runnin' the Fourth o' July, I think it was, runnin' a big gray fox. Across the road runnin' right down 'side this culvert, oh, 'bout like that. [Unintelligible.] You've seen it where, that's what, briar, you know, you know briar up under there, you know, know what I'm talkin' 'bout – these ol' . . . where . . . got them stickers on, 'bout like that [holds up his finger], 'bout that size, got that runner, big runner to 'em. And just had the place solid.

And we had a fox under there, and got him under there 'bout three o'clock, and he stayed there till it got daylight, he stayed under there to daylight. The road on east side o' that place.

And daylight come and them ol' feet comin' out from under round there drove her all buggy. He just walked in them briars. Place he could get in, you'd just see him every while just walkin', just walkin'. You could hear that gyp now smell that fox. He got him hot, he just walk in them briars.

That little gyp come up in now, and she come up, man, there, like this fox, far like to the middle o' this pickup, quite that far – come out, shot out from under there, wasn't long before she come out just sprawled on her belly.

There she is, right there. There she is right there. [To dog] Yeah, come over here.

(Recorded Canton, Texas, July 31, 1971)

In the second encounter there are three participants, only two of whom are heard in this excerpt: Homer Townsend and Herman Smith. Townsend's son is interested in Smith's dogs, but his father does the talking.

Townsend: Will them ol' dogs you got catch a rabbit?

Smith: Yeah.

Townsend: Really get up there and catch one?

Smith: Yes sir. I'd buy another one that'll outrun 'em.

Townsend: Well, a man told me a while ago they wouldn't hardly *run* a rabbit.

Smith: I tell you what I'll do. I'll take the man out here and *show* him. That's all I can do. . . . that's the *best* way, is to take him out and show him. I'll buy another 'un that can run with 'em . . . uh, keep 'em or sell or buy another 'un that could run with 'em, see. . . .

Townsend: [Interrupts] He's interested in some dogs, some greyhounds, and, uh, that man says they wouldn't hardly run a rabbit.

Smith: [Angrily] I'll *show* you! That's all I can do. You know me, I don't *lie* about these dogs. I tried 'em out, see, I tried them dogs out before I ever bought 'em, see. And I do the *coon* dogs thataway. I wouldn't give a dime for nary a dog I didn't know on this ground until I hunted him.

I sold one last . . . uh . . . summer and the man asked me what I'd take. I said, "I won't even price him till you go huntin'." I said, "I sell mine in the *woods!*" And when we went huntin', he treed three coons. Come out, and he said, "Whatcha want for that dog?" I said two-fifty. And he went countin' out them twenty-dollar bills.

I got a little ol' gyp out there I've had three years. And she's three years old – she's been treein' coons ever since she was a year old! And she's still in my pen! And I got one o' her puppies mated to that 'un yonder . . . that's the one over there. Took him out the other day, just started trainin' him, you know.

That's the reason I got them greyhounds, 'cause I can see 'em, see? I can't hear a thing outta this ear. I gotta go with somebody and they got a bunch of trash and. . . . No, somebody got one to run with 'em, I'll buy 'em this morning.

Townsend: [Leaving] Well, we'll talk to you a little bit . . . after a while.

Smith: [Loudly] I'll take 'em out here and *show* you! That's the way I am. I don't lie about these dogs. I ain't . . . I don't believe in it.

I bought a dog here 'bout three or four months ago down here from an ol' man and ended high nigh walkin' him! And he was tellin' me about that dog, trainin' young dogs and this 'n' that, and I give him thirty dollars for it, and I *give* him to that little boy down there. That hound don't tree. I *give* him to him. I wouldn't lie to him, I *give* it to him! I don't lie about it. I'll buy 'em on the tree or sell 'em on the tree, I don't care about the money. I don't lie about these dogs. You hear anything very long and you'll say it's all right, you know what I mean?

(Recorded by Donna West, Canton, Texas, November 1, 1970)

For our purposes, two features stand out from these excerpts. First, the participants clearly devote a considerable amount of interactional attention to the issue of truthfulness and lying; and, second, one of the devices they resort to in addressing this issue is telling stories. Anyone who is at all familiar with hound-dog men, coon hunters, or otherwise, will feel no surprise at hearing they have some involvement in lying and storytelling. Georg Simmel suggests that "sociological structures differ profoundly according to the measure of lying which operates in them" (1950:312), and coon hunting certainly ranks fairly high on this scale.

To an audience familiar with coon hunters, the association between lying and coon hunting is so well established that it constitutes an expressive resource for performance. The humorous monologue of the featured speaker at a Fourth of July celebration in Pekin, Indiana – an area near the Indiana–Kentucky border that is full of coon hunters – included the following introduction to a series of hunting stories:

> You know, now, somebody's accused me of lying, and I told somebody one time how bad it hurt me to lie, and they said, "you must be in awful pain, then, buddy." But I have had to lie some just to get by, you understand? I didn't want to lie, I was pushed into it. I done a lot of coon hunting, and when you go out with a bunch of coon hunters you got to lie just to stay with 'em.
>
> I can see by looking that there's no coon hunters in this audience today. I'm glad I did, I didn't want to insult anybody. But when you get out there in the field with a bunch of coon hunters, and get you a chew of tobacco in your mouth, and the dogs start running, you better start telling some lies, or you won't be out there long.
> (Byron Crawford, recorded Pekin, Indiana, July 4, 1978)

Or, as summed up for me with artful succinctness by a Texas coon hunter, "any man who keeps more'n one hound'll lie to you."

One type of lying associated with coon hunting, and of long-standing interest to folklorists, is the tall tale, the traditional tale of lying and exaggeration. Hunting has always been a privileged domain for tall tales: *The Types of the Folktale* (Thompson 1961) established the hunting tale as a special subgroup of tales of lying (types 1890–1909), and the standard American tall-tale collections are full of hunting windies (see Baughman 1966: types 1890–1909 and motifs X1100–1199, and references therein).

Traditional tall tales are told at Canton, but not often. Since the regulars have heard them over and over again, they tend largely to save them for newcomers not yet fully integrated into the coon-hunting fraternity (cf. Toelken 1979:112). The following tale, widely recorded, was addressed by a veteran hunter to a nineteen-year-old novice in the group:

This ol' boy, he had him a coon dog. He had him a little coon [hide-] stretcher, looked like a piece of wire, V-shaped. He'd bring it out of the house, he had that coon dog, and it'd go out in the woods, kill him a coon, bring it back to the house, and all that boy had to do was just skin that coon out, put on that stretcher and skin. He was doing that for about two or three years, and was plum proud of his dog, and everything, and was telling everybody in town how good that dog was.

One day his mama told him to take the ironing board outside to fix it; there was something wrong with it. That dog seen that ironing board and that dog hadn't showed up yet.[1] (Recorded Canton, Texas, June 2, 1973)

Tall tales such as this one play upon the generic expectations of another type of story which is ubiquitous among hound-dog men: narratives of personal experience about the special qualities and hunting prowess of particular dogs. The story of the dog and the ironing board/hide-stretcher followed closely on the heels of this one:

A: I run a coon down the creek back down home at Fred's a couple weeks
     ago. . . .

B: Yeah?

A: And I couldn't get him out, couldn't get in there to him, so Speck and I
     got . . . I caught Speck to lead him off now, "let's go, Speck."

     Went on down there, struck another coon and treed it. He jumped it out, and old Speck just whirled and left there, and I didn't know where in hell that sumbitch went.

     First time I heard him opened up back down on the tree. He went back there and checked the hole, that coon had come out and he treed that sumbitch down there [laughing].

C: Yeah.

D: Sure did. Dog's smart.

A: That durn coon came outa that hole. He went and treed that coon.

C: Yeah. That's what me and Bud done one night. Treed one down there. . . .

A: [Interrupting] He was thinkin' about that coon, wasn't he?

(Recorded Canton, Texas, August 1, 1971)

Stories like this one dominate the sociable encounters of coon hunters wherever they come together, including the dog-trading grounds at Canton. These accounts stick close to the actual world of coon hunting and to the range of the possible – though not, in the best of them, to the ordinary. The extraor-

---

[1] Baughman (1966), motif X1215.8 (aa): Master shows dog a skin-stretching board; the dog brings in a raccoon just the size of the board. Master's mother puts ironing board outside one day. The dog never returns.

dinary, the "reportable" in Labov's terms, is necessary if a personal narrative is to hold the listener's attention (Labov and Fanshel 1977:105). A dog like old Speck that can remind itself of a piece of unfinished business and go back to finish it off after treeing another coon is special, though believable. Why not, then, a dog that will catch a coon on order, to fit his master's hide-stretcher? The more common story of personal experience, told straightforwardly as truth, contextualizes the tall tale; it contributes to the latter's humorous effect by establishing a set of generic expectations that the tall tale can bend exaggeratedly out of shape. The effect is reciprocal, of course: The obvious exaggeration of the tall tale creates an aura of lying that colors the "true" stories as well.

When we juxtapose the personal narrative and the tall tale, actually two dimensions of "lying" become apparent. First, the unusual but not impossible events of the former are transformed into the exaggeratedly implausible events of the latter. Thus tall tales are lies, insofar as what they report as having happened either did not happen or could not have happened.

There is more, though. The tall tale presented above is told in the third person, which distances it somewhat from the narrator, and contrasts with the characteristic use of the first-person voice in the personal narrative. A common feature of tall-tale style, however, is also the use of the first person (Brunvand 1978:136–7), either directly ("I had an old coon dog that would go out in the woods. . . .") or as a link between the narrator and the third-person protagonist ("I knew an old boy, he had a coon dog . . ."). This device occurs in the second traditional tale we will consider below. When the first-person voice is employed, a second dimension of "lying" comes into play. The use of the first person brings the tall tale closer to personal narrative; it allows the story to masquerade for a while as a "true" personal narrative, until the realization that what is being reported is impossible shatters the illusion. In other words, these first-person tall tales are what Goffman calls "fabrications," "the intentional effort of one or more individuals to manage activity so that a party of one or more others will be induced to have a false belief about what it is that is going on" (1974:83). What appears to be going on is an account of actual events; what is really going on is a lie masquerading as such an account – a double lie. The man who tells such a tale in the third person is a liar; the man who tells it in the first person is a tricky liar, a con man. Thus two potential dimensions of "lying" enter into the expressive ambience of coon hunters: outright lies and fabrications.

As I have noted, though, traditional tall tales are not very common at Canton. But even without them, the aura of lying persists around the personal dog stories because, although recounted as true, they are susceptible to creative exaggeration, another dimension of "lying," for at least two major reasons. First, like all natural sociable interaction, the encounters of coon hunters are at base about the construction and negotiation of personal identity. In them, sociable narratives are a vehicle for the encoding and presentation of information about oneself in order to construct a personal and social image (Bauman 1972a). In Watson and Potter's apt formulation, "social interaction gives form to the image of self and the image of the other; it gives validity and continuity to the identifications which are the source of an individual's self-esteem" (1962:246). The way to establish that you are a good coon hunter is to show that you have good hounds and are thus knowledgeable about quality dogs – even more so if you have trained them yourself. Thus, because hunting stories are instruments for identity building, for self-aggrandizement (Labov and Waletzky 1967:34), there is a built-in impulse to exaggerate the prowess of one's dogs with hyperbole ("When he trees, hell, if you ain't give out, you're plum gonna get him of starvation before he comes away from there"), or by selection (omitting mention of the faults of a dog you're bragging on) as a means of enhancing one's own image (cf. Gilsenan 1976:191). This tendency toward "stretching the truth," as it is often called, has been widely reported in men's sociable encounters (see, e.g., Bauman 1972a; Bethke 1976: Biebuyck-Goetz 1977; Cothran 1974; Tallman 1975). It is one more factor that gives hound-dog men the reputation of being liars.

The other factor that promotes the expressive elaboration of the hound and hunting story is that, whatever its referential and rhetorical functions, it constitutes a form of verbal art. That is, it is characteristically *performed*, subject to evaluation, both as truth and as art for the skill and effectiveness with which it is told (Bauman 1977b:11). The aesthetic considerations of artistic performance may demand the embellishment or manipulation – if not the sacrifice – of the literal truth in the interests of greater dynamic tension, formal elegance, surprise value, contrast, or other elements that contribute to excellence in performance in this subculture. "Stretching the truth," which chiefly exaggerates and selects, is not exactly the same as the outright lying of the tall tale. Nevertheless, although the two activities can be terminologically distinguished to point up the contrast between them, they are usually merged, and the term "lying," in an unmarked sense, is used to label both (see diagram). Fabrication, our third analytically distinguished type of lying, has no folk label.

For these reasons, then, some expectation of lying attends the telling of these stories about special dogs and memorable hunts. Realizing this, the tellers frequently resort to various means of validating their accounts (cf. Ben-Amos 1976:30–2). These range from verbal formulas like "I guarantee," to the testimony of witnesses (as in the above story), to offers to demonstrate the dog in action. One man concluded a lengthy story about the hunting prowess of his hound as follows:

> You don't believe it, take and let your dogs run a coon loose, and I'll lead her, anybody tonight, anybody got their damn good cold-nose dogs, and if she don't run that coon and tree that coon, it's gonna be somethin' that ain't never happened. She'll run that sum-bitch till by god, she'll tree that sumbitch. (Recorded Canton, Texas, August 1, 1971)

But even such emphatic attempts at validation often contain elements that subtly undermine the intended effect. In the statement just quoted, the owner backs up his previous claim about his dog's ability to follow a cold trail to the tree by stating that it has *never* failed to do so. Whereas the dog in question did in fact have a far higher success rate than most others, both the owner and several of the onlookers knew of times when it had failed, as any dog must once in a while. So, despite these attempts at validation, the expectation persists that hound-dog men will lie when talking about their dogs.

Occasionally, among intimates, someone may make a playful thrust at discrediting a story. To cite one example from Canton, a man, spotting an old friend who was giving an account of a recent hunt to a circle of fellow hunters, called out as he approached, "What you doin', lyin' to these people?" This is joking, however. The interesting and noteworthy thing about the sociable storytelling of hound-dog men is that, although it is strongly recognized as susceptible to lying, the lying is overwhelmingly licensed as part of the fundamental ethos of sociability. That is, by not challenging the truthfulness of another's stories, one may reasonably expect to be accorded the same license in presenting one's own image-building narratives and crafting one's own artful performances. Then too, it is only susceptibility we are talking about; not every personal narrative about dogs and hunting involves lying, nor is it always clear or consciously recognized as to which do and which do not. There is merely a persistent sense that every story might. To call another man a liar in this context, then, is to threaten his "face," with some risk and no possible advantage to oneself; whereas to give apparent acceptance to his accounts is to store up interactional credit toward the unchallenged acceptance of one's own tales.

Hunting tall tales and ordinary dog stories do not exhaust the repertoire of storytelling at Canton. The special character of First Monday for the hunters who attend is that it is an occasion for dog trading; not surprisingly, then, trading itself constitutes an important conversational resource for those who gather there. Like the hunting tall tales, some of the trading stories are traditional fictions, part of the national – even international – treasury of lore about shrewd trades, deceptive bargains, gullibility, and guile. To underscore his observations about a smart fellow trader, a dog jockey from Oklahoma who almost never misses a First Monday at Canton told the following story:

> And they're smart, too. I know an ol' boy, by god, he fell on a damn scheme to make some money, you know? Got hisself a bunch o' damn dog pills. 'Stead o' them damn . . . he called 'em "smart pills," you know, and by god, he'd sell them damn things, and an ol' boy'd come along, and he'd sell 'em a little to 'em, and tell 'em how smart they'd make 'em, you know, an' he'd get a *dollar* a piece for 'em.
>
> An ol' boy come along, and he sold him one.
>
> He said, "hell, I don't feel any smarter than I did."
>
> He said, "I found sometimes when you're pretty dumb it takes several of 'em, by god, to get you smartened up."
>
> He bought another one, took it, stood around there a few minutes, and said, "now, I ain't no smarter than I was."
>
> "Boy," he says, "you're somethin', you're just pretty dumb. You . . . you've got to take four or five for you."
>
> Well, he bought another one, took it, so he stood around, and he said, "man, them things ain't helping me a damn bit."
>
> He said, "I told you, you was pretty dumb." He said, "by god, you're gonna have to take another one."
>
> So he bought another one, by god, and he took that son of a bitch and rolled it around in his damn hand, and he reached up to taste it, and he said, "that tastes just like dog shit."
>
> He said, "boy, now you smartenin' up."[2] (Recorded Canton, Texas, June 5, 1977)

Let us examine this story in the light of our discussion thus far. Linked to the conversation that precedes it, and opened in the first person ("I know an ol' boy . . ."), the story appears at first to be a conventional personal narrative of the kind that is told as true. Ultimately, it is revealed as a humorous fiction. Like the traditional tall tale told in the first person, then, this story is both a lie and a fabrication. Its content, however, endows it with an additional dimension of deception. The trader here has clearly swindled the dupe by playing on his expectation that the "smart pills" would make him wiser by virtue of their medicinal powers. That, after all, is how pills work. The trader, of course, has made no such explicit claim. He has merely advertised his wares as "smart pills," and they do in fact make the dupe smarter – he wises up to the fact that he has been paying a dollar each for pellets of dog dung.

---

[2] Thompson (1955–8), motif K114.3.1: *Virtue of oracular pill proved*. The dupe takes it. "It is dog's dung," he says, spitting it out. The trickster says that he is telling the truth and demands pay.

This story is one of a type of traditional tale in which the shrewd trader, although not actually telling an untruth – and thus not lying in a limited, literal sense – lies in effect nevertheless, at least in the sense set forth by Charles Morris (1946:261): "lying is the deliberate use of signs to misinform someone, that is, to produce in someone the belief that certain signs are true which the producer himself believes to be false." In the story above, the trader's ploy is actually a kind of fabrication, insofar as he induces the dupe to believe that he is taking pills that will affect him medicinally, whereas in fact such effect as they have is the result of his realization that this belief is false. The tale thus underscores in expressive form the semiparadoxical fact that traders can lie by telling the truth. The "smart pills" deception is at least arguably a "benign fabrication," in Goffman's terms (1974:87), leading as it does to the enlightenment of the dupe. However, "exploitive fabrications" (ibid.:103) also abound in this body of folklore and, as we shall see, in actual trading as well.

My impression, unverified by conclusive data, is that traditional tales about trading, like the one I have just presented, are less generally familiar to the population of the dog grounds at Canton than are the traditional tall tales about dogs and hunting. The latter are appropriate, in a general sense, whenever coon hunters come together sociably, whereas the former are more likely to be familiar to those with a regular involvement in trading, a much smaller group. In the setting of a First Monday, though, trading tales are highly appropriate, and I have heard more traditional stories about trading than traditional tall tales about hunting on the dog grounds.

Still more common are personal narratives about trades in which the teller himself was involved. Some of these, interestingly, are about being taken. Dog trading is, after all, a contest, and even the canny trader can be bested occasionally, as in the following account:

A: That's that little Trigg [a breed of hound] I's tellin' you about.
B: I bought one o' them one time, Cal, was the funniest thing I got in. When I swapped for her, and give some money, in Texarkana, old boy said, "I guarantee her." Said, "she's one of the finest coon dogs I've ever had in the woods in my life."

      I carried that dog home, I pitched her out, first thing she hit was a deer. I think a day or two later, I finally found her. And I mean she wouldn't run *one* thing on earth but a deer, not anything.

      So I carried her back to Texarkana and just give her away. Yes sir. And *five* minutes after the boy drove off with that dog, a guy drove up and said, "do you know where I can find a deer dog anywhere for sale?"
C & D: [Laugh]

B: I'll bet he hadn't got two mile outa town, when . . .

D: [Interrupting] Outa town dog and all?

B: Yeah. Ain't no tellin' what he'd give for the dog, and she was perfect. I mean she was a straight deer dog. Wouldn't run nothin' else. But that's my luck.

(Recorded Canton, Texas, August 1, 1971)

In this story, the teller loses out not once, but twice. He is victimized by being lied to outright by another trader – note the inevitable preoccupation with lying – and then compounds the problem by giving away the deer dog, worthless to a coon hunter, moments before he is presented with a golden opportunity to sell it at a handsome profit. Still, he is philosophical about it; he introduces the story as the *funniest* experience he has had with Trigg hounds and chalks up the whole experience to luck.

Whereas admitting that one has been taken in a trade might seem to expose one to some risk of losing face, the risk is apparently offset by the reportability and performance value of a good story. And, after all, it did take an outright lie on the trader's part to accomplish the deception. Moreover, any trader worth his salt has plenty of stories about how he bested someone else in a trade by the exercise of wit, cleverness, or deception. The same man who lost out twice on the deer dog told the following story, recounting a classic example of the short con, a fabrication par excellence.

> Last time I went over to Canton, I had a dog I called Blackjack. He was just about as sorry a dog as I ever had owned. He wouldn't do nothin' but eat. Take him huntin' and he lay out under the pickup.
>
> So I decided I'd take him over to Canton, and I did, and I met a friend of mine over there, named Ted Haskell, out o' Corsicana. I told Ted, I said, "now, you go up that alley up yonder and meet me 'bout half-way where they's tradin' dogs yonder, and then we'll introduce ourselves. You . . . we'll . . . sell this dog, and I'll give you half what I get outa it."
>
> I met ol' Ted, and he says, "well, ol' Blackjack," he says, "I haven't had a coon race since I sold him," he says, "where'd you get him?"
>
> "I got him over to Palestine."
>
> "Well, I declare, I wisht I had him back," he says, "what are you askin' for him?"
>
> I said, "I'll take thirty dollars."
>
> Well, they began to gather 'round and listen and listen. We kept talkin' 'bout him. He'd brag on Blackjack. And finally, an ol' boy eased up and called me off and says, "I'll give twenty dollars for him."

And I said, "Well, pay me." Well, he paid me.

Course I told Mr. Haskell mighty glad I'd met him, and he turned and went one way, and I went the other way, and we met at the pickup and divided the money. I come home, and he come back to Corsicana.

So I'm sure that man felt about like I did when I bought him, 'cause he wasn't worth carryin' a-huntin'. (Recorded by Thomas A. Green, Blooming Grove, Texas, May 31, 1968)

Stories like this one manifest a significant ambivalence about lying and other swindles, especially about lying – whether outright lying, stretching the truth, or fabrication – in conducting the trading itself. As I have noted, dog trading is viewed by the confirmed traders as a game of strategy in which, like many other games of strategy, deception occupies a central and accepted place. There is a long tradition in American folklore and popular literature of admiration for the shrewd trader, from the Yankee peddler to the Southern horse trader, who makes his way through the world by wit and words, part of "the traditional sympathy which storytellers have for rascals and crooks" (Benjamin 1969:106; cf. Dorson 1959:47–8; Ferris 1977; Green 1968, 1972). The numerous entries in Baughman's *Type and Motif-Index of the Folktales of England and North America* (1966) under K134, Deceptive horse sale (or trade), as well as such literary pieces as the horse trader in Longstreet's *Georgia Scenes* or the recent popular collections of horse-trading tales by Ben Green (1968, 1972; see also Welsch 1981), suggest that Americans enjoy hearing about shrewd traders and therefore, at some level at least, accept their crooked dealings (cf. Boatright 1973:146). The interplay between the trader's verbal skill in trading and his verbal skill as a storyteller is probably significant here; the two are complementary aspects of his overall image as quick-witted and shrewd, one who manipulates men and situations – whether trading encounters or social gatherings – to his own advantage (cf. Benjamin 1969:101). Good traders are not reluctant self-publicists; one Canton regular told me with obvious pride: "I'll tell you what you can do. You can put me right out there on that road, barefooted, if it wasn't too hot, and before I get home, I'll have a pair of shoes, I want to tell you."

Nevertheless, whereas chess, for example, is unequivocally and only a game, in which such strategic deception as may occur is completely contained within the play frame, dog trading is not so unambiguous. Whereas trading is certainly engaged in as play by many of the participants at Canton, the play frame is almost never overtly acknowledged. The only instances I observed that were openly marked as play were framed by such obviously inappropriate offers as five dollars plus a toothless old dog for a proven hound in prime condition. Otherwise, the public construction placed upon the trading encounter depicts it as a serious business transaction, and it is *always* susceptible to being understood as such by one or both participants.

Here is the crux of the matter. The traditional American ideal demands, if not absolute honesty in business transactions, at least the maintenance of the public fiction that the participants are telling the truth (cf. Simmel 1950:314). Thus lying does not accord with the public construction of a dog-trading transaction, nor is it consistent with the actual understanding of those who consider a dog trade straight business, not a game. The trader who lies about a dog during the conduct of a trade may see himself and be seen by some other traders as a master player, gulling the marks as they deserve, but he may also be despised as a swindler who cheats honest people. No harm is done by telling stories about shrewd or crooked trades – indeed, such accounts may be relished for their performance value – but actually hoodwinking someone is a different matter. It makes the difference between Goffman's benign and exploitative fabrications (1974:87, 103).

At the same time, therefore, that a trader is telling a well-formed and entertaining story in which he beats someone by a classic confidence trick, he may also be at pains to disavow any dishonesty. The veteran trader who unloaded Blackjack by trickery and obviously relished telling about it had just a few minutes before beginning his story made a gesture at resolving the moral dilemma by framing his trading swindles as the excesses of youth: "Most men my age won't lie about a dog; but just before you get to my age, they'll lie and tell you any kinda tale just to get to sell you a dog."

Having explored the relationship between lying and storytelling among the dog traders at Canton to this point, we can now return to the excerpts from the trading encounters with which we began our exploration. The strong preoccupation with lying and storytelling that characterizes both encounters should be relatively more comprehensible in light of the preceding discussion.

The rich expressive tradition of storytelling associated with hound-dog men and dog traders – the tales of hunting and trading and the personal narratives about both activities – as well as the conception of dog trading as a game c ˆ strategy in which the goal is often to get rid of a worthless dog at a profit help endow dog trading at Canton with a considerable aura of lying and de ception. These expressive forms both reflect and sustain the sense that mis representation of one sort or another permeates the institution, and many par ticipants can confirm from first-hand experience that lying is indeed a factor to be reckoned with. It is not at all surprising that parties on both sides of a dog trade should enter the transaction anticipating that the opposite party might lie about a dog and expect to be lied to in return. At the same time, either man (both parties if a trade is involved, only the seller if it is to be a cash sale) might in fact be ready and willing to lie to unload a dog. Yet even if one is ready to lie, to acknowledge as much is impossible; it would violate the public construction that dog trading is an honest business transaction and would very likely undermine the interactional foundation of the trading relationship itself.

The strategy that emerges from the expectations and conventions of dog trading is that one should take pains during an actual transaction to *dispel* the aura of lying that surrounds it. The most direct means of doing so is by explicit insistence on one's truthfulness and by disavowal of lying (cf. Bakhtin 1968:162). In the encounters under examination, both John Moore and Herman Smith employ this means of establishing their trustworthiness. John Moore volunteers early in the encounter: "I try to be fair with a man 'bout a dog. Tell the truth about a dog, tell you what he'll do. If there's any fault to him, I wanna tell the man." And then, employing the powerful rhetorical device of identification (Burke 1969:20–3), Moore puts himself in Byers's position: "If I get a dog from a man, if there's any fault to him, I want him to tell me." A little later, to validate the information he is providing about his dogs, he insists: "If I tell you somep'n 'bout a dog, I'm not gon' misrepresent him. Not gonna misrepresent him." In the second encounter, Herman Smith is rather seriously challenged by Homer Townsend; he reiterates with some vehemence throughout the encounter, "I don't lie about these dogs!" These are all disclaimers of outright lying or of stretching the truth by selection or distortion. I have not recorded or observed any instances in which a participant disavowed pulling off a fabrication, although it is conceivable that such disavowals might occur.

Another means of establishing one's veracity in a trading encounter is to offer to let the dogs prove the claims made for them, just as the tellers of dog stories do in sociable encounters. This is Herman Smith's main thrust; he offers repeatedly to "take 'em out here and show you." He also resorts to the identificational strategy of putting himself in the place of the buyer. When he is buying dogs, he tries them out: "I wouldn't give a dime for nary a dog I didn't know on this ground until I hunted him." By trying out the dogs he is offering before having bought them, Smith has, in effect, already acted on Townsend's behalf, and Townsend is safe in buying them now.

For our purposes, perhaps the most interesting means by which the dog traders seek to establish and substantiate their identities as honest men is in telling stories. If we examine these stories, we see that they are closely related to the sociable narratives discussed at length earlier in this chapter – specifically, to personal narratives about the performance of particular dogs and to personal narratives about trading experiences.

Three narratives appear in the excerpt from the first trading encounter – two told by John Moore and one very minimal one told by Mr. Byers. Moore clearly tells his first story, about being victimized in a trade by buying some puppies that the seller falsely assures him had had their shots, as a rhetorical strategy to convey his negative attitudes toward a trader who would tell an outright lie about a dog. By implication, he emphasizes his own trustworthiness in a context wherein trickery and deceit are widespread. Moore's central rhetorical purpose is to distance himself from dog traders who lie, and his story is obviously and strongly adapted to that purpose. Much of his narrative is given over to establishing this polarization (Labov 1979) between the dishonest trader and Moore himself, as customer. The trader's lie is doubly destructive because it was both unnecessary, since Moore was going to buy the dogs whether or not they had had their shots, and cruel, since it resulted in the death of the dogs. The evaluative dimension of the narrative is heavily elaborated, both through repetition (both the query to the trader about whether the puppies were vaccinated and the narrative report of those queries are repeated) and lexical intensifiers (emotion-laden words like "swore," "hate," "begged") (Labov and Waletzky 1967:37–8). The point is that Moore gave the trader ample and repeated opportunity to tell the truth, but he remained firm in his lie; and everyone suffered as a result, even the liar himself, since the death of the puppies brought him remorse ("he hate that he didn't tell us . . .").

Byers too has been taken in a trade. He comes back with his account of having traded once for two dogs that were supposed to be good fox dogs and then discovering that the "sumbitches wouldn't run a *rabbit.*" This story establishes that he has already been victimized at least once in a trade and, by implication, that he does not intend to let it happen again. As he is not the one whose honesty is on the line, however, having no dog to trade, his story is rather minimal – just long enough to make his point, without attempting to be strongly persuasive. Still, there is not a clause in his narrative that lacks a clearly evaluative element.

Moore goes on to reaffirm his bona fides by mentioning his satisfied customers, including "some rich, up-to-date people." Then, picking up on Byers's apparent interest in fox dogs, Moore points out a fox dog among his own string, and proceeds to tell an extended story about her prowess in a recent hunt in order to build up her credentials – a sales pitch in narrative form. Stories of this kind are especially motivated during trading transactions because one cannot tell from merely looking at a dog what its hunting abilities are. Straightforward enumeration of the dog's qualities could also get the information across, but corroborating narratives, convincingly told, may add verisimilitude to the seller's claims. Skill in storytelling may thus enhance the overall rhetorical power of the sales pitch. One must maintain a delicate balance, however, because stories are also considered vehicles for creative or duplicitous misrepresentation. Hence the usefulness of combining such narratives with additional claims to honesty, as Moore does both directly and by telling his story about a dishonest dog trader in order to distance himself from such practices. As the one offering the dogs, Moore has to tell stories that are persuasive enough to establish both his honesty, as in the first story, and the dog's quality, persistence, toughness, and so on, as in the second. In sociable interaction, there is no immediate negative consequence if your audience does not accept the truth of your story; in trading encounters, others must accept your story sufficiently to be persuaded to *act* on it (it is hoped by trading for or buying your dog).

The second excerpt contains two stories, both told by Herman Smith, the man with the dogs. Townsend has rather seriously challenged him with offering dogs that won't perform. Smith accordingly counters with a story to demonstrate that, far from being willing to risk a customer's dissatisfaction or skepticism, he would actually *refuse* to conclude a sale until the dog has proven itself in the woods. This is not just honesty, it's superhonesty. Smith's second story is in the same vein: Having been taken in by an unscrupulous trader who lied about the treeing ability of a dog, Smith would not himself stoop to selling the worthless hound, but gave it away to a little boy. Any man who gives dogs to little boys can't be all bad. Here is another instance of extreme polarization between the dishonest trader and the honest man: The unscrupulous trader places profit over honesty, whereas Smith values honesty over profit ("I don't care about the money. I don't lie about these dogs"). Just so there is no question about his own honorable values, he repeats the relevant points again and again.

Honesty . . .	over profit
I wouldn't lie to him.	I *gave* him to that little boy down there.
I don't lie about it.	I *give* him to him!
I don't lie about these dogs.	I *give* it to him!

Interestingly, this story compromises one of Smith's earlier claims to Townsend – that he himself tries out all the dogs he acquires before buying them. If he had done so in this case, he would not have had a worthless dog fobbed off on him. But it is more important to tell an emphatic story for its rhetorical effect than to worry about a minor inconsistency like this. Should Townsend pick up on it, this inconsistency could undermine Smith's claims to scrupulous honesty.

This second story of Smith's so closely parallels the story of the deer dog, discussed earlier, that a brief comparison can highlight certain significant differences generated by the differing contexts in which they occur and their respective functions within these contexts. In both stories the narrator acquires a dog from someone who lies to get rid of it and then, discovering that the dog does not perform as expected, gives it away. The story of the deer dog, told for entertainment in sociable interaction, is connected to the discourse that precedes it solely by the fact that the dog in question was a Trigg hound, and the previous speaker had pointed out a Trigg in his own string of dogs. No more is needed for the story to be appropriate in this sociable context. The extra twist at the end of the story, in which a customer appears for the dog immediately after it has been given away, makes the tale unusual and endows it with entertainment value. There is credit to be gained, as a performer, in telling it. The event sequence consists of six principal episodes, most of which have subepisodes:

1. Trading for the dog in the expectation that it was a coon dog
2. Taking it home
3. Taking it on a disastrous trial hunt, in which it turns out to be a deer dog
4. Having to search for the now apparently worthless dog
5. Returning to Texarkana to give it away
6. Being approached by someone looking for a deer hound exactly like the one just given away

The evaluative dimension of the story serves to highlight the reportability of the experience, the humor and irony of the situation.

Herman Smith's story, however, is more strongly motivated and rooted in its conversational context. Smith's prospective customers are leaving, apparently because they don't believe his dogs are any good, and he is very concerned to establish his trustworthiness as a dog trader. The narrative line of the story is minimal:

1. Trading for the dog
2. Discovering that it won't perform as promised
3. Giving it away

More important by far is the rhetorical impact. The rhetorical power of the story resides in the fact that, unlike the unscrupulous trader, Smith spurned the opportunity to swindle someone else with a worthless dog; instead, he gave it away to the little boy. This is the point that he emphasizes most strongly in his story. Most of the work of the narrative, the thrust of its heavy evaluative dimension, aims at a polarization between the dishonest trader and the honorable narrator. Note, however, that this story, like those of John Moore and Mr. Byers, does also involve a trader who is not as honest as Smith presents himself to be, one who lies outright about a dog. Thus we come full circle: The very story that is told in the course of a trading encounter to dispel any suspicion of the trader's dishonesty reinforces the aura of lying that surrounds trading in general. Any man who keeps more'n one hound'll lie to you.

Dog trading at Canton First Monday brings together and merges two important figures in American tradition, the hunter and the trader. Both are strongly associated with storytelling as subjects and performers, and both are major exponents of the widely noted (though not exclusively) American predilection for expressive lying. Since at least the time when a distinctive body of American folk humor first emerged during the early years of the American republic, the hunter and the trader have occupied a privileged place in American folklore. Dog trading at Canton is a thriving contemporary incarnation of this American folk tradition. The tall tales and personal narratives of its participants place them in unbroken continuity with the generations of hunters, traders, and storytellers that have given American folklore some of its most distinctive characteristics. At the same time, First Monday dog trading offers a richly textured arena for the ethnographic investigation of the nuances of expressive lying, the negotiation of truthfulness and lying as action and evaluation in the conduct of social life.

The narratives that are the instruments of these negotiations do not fall into clear-cut categories of factual and fictional, truthful and lying, believable and incredible, but rather interweave in a complex contextual web that leaves these issues constantly in doubt, ever susceptible to strategic manipulation whenever a trade is joined.[3]

[3]   An earlier version of this chapter appeared in Bauman (1981).

3

"WE WAS ALWAYS PULLIN' JOKES"

The management of point of view in personal experience narratives

Fabrications – both enacted and narrated – represent a fertile field for the exploration of the interrelationships binding together the narrated event, the narrative itself, and the event in which the narrative is recounted, as we saw in the preceding chapter. This chapter pursues this same problem from another direction, with reference to a further class of fabrications that has traditionally represented a productive resource for storytellers, namely, practical jokes.

There has been a notable and productive convergence of interest in recent years among linguists, sociologists, and folklorists around the nature and function of oral narratives of personal experience. William Labov has taken the lead among linguists in pursuing this subject of inquiry, using the texts of oral narratives of personal experience in the classic linguistic tradition as extended forms of natural discourse, but extending his analysis of structure beyond sentence grammar to encompass the narrative as a whole (Labov 1972, 1982; Labov and Waletzky 1967). From the standpoint of sociology, Erving Goffman has examined stories of personal experience as important instruments in the operation of the interaction order, including the presentation of self and the construction and communication of a sense of situational reality (Goffman 1959, 1974). And among folklorists, Sandra Stahl has directed the attention of her colleagues in a number of significant publications to this most ubiquitous of contemporary narrative forms, stressing the continuities between personal experience stories and other genres of folk narrative (Stahl 1977a,b, 1983).

All three scholars use the term "personal experience" to designate the kinds of narratives in which they are interested. Labov calls them "narratives of personal experience" (1972), Stahl "personal experience stories" (1983), and Goffman "tale or anecdote [or] replaying" of "personal experience" (1974:504). These are natural enough designations for the stories under examination, but I want to bring to the fore two related implications of the terms that have not been much reflected upon in relation to these forms as narrative, namely, that "personal experience" implies both (1) a particular class of reported events, and (2) a particular point of view. That is, the event recounted in these narratives is purportedly one in which the person telling the story was originally personally involved, and the point of view from which the event is recounted is that of the narrator by virtue of his or her participation in that event.

Notwithstanding that the very term "personal experience narrative" incorporates these assumptions, the management of point of view and the relationship between the story and the narrated event in these narratives have not been subjected to direct empirical investigation and analysis (but see Schrager 1983). This is all the more noteworthy in that the relationship between story and event and the management of narrative information through the manipulation of point of view have long been recognized by literary theorists as critical dimensions of narrative construction. In the works cited above, however, these matters are either adumbrated but not investigated, or are rendered unproblematic by a priori assumption or by methodological constraints on the data.

One of the narratives of personal experience recently analyzed by Labov (1982:223–4), for example, recounts an event in which the narrator's experiential involvement was solely as third-person *witness* to the central actions, whereas other significant portions of the narrated event occurred out of her sight. Yet this story is presented by Labov with two others in which there is an intense, unified, first-person focus on the narrator as protagonist in the original event. Are all three stories equivalent as narratives of personal experience? Labov's formal and functional analysis of the group does not extend to the crucial differences in the ways the respective stories are made.

Stahl does distinguish two essential kinds of personal experience narratives and narrators in terms that suggest differential management of point of view: "other-oriented" and "self-oriented." "Other-oriented narrators underplay their personal role in the story to emphasize the extraordinary nature of things that happen in the tale" (Stahl 1983:270), whereas " 'self-oriented tellers' delight in weaving fairly elaborate tales that build upon their own self-images and emphasize their own actions as either humorous or exemplary" (Stahl 1983:270). The types are illustrated by examples, but Stahl does not analyze the distinction between them in formal terms.

Goffman (1974), for his part, comes closer than the others to a recognition of the literary problematics of point of view and the relationship of personal narrative to narrated event, even citing the works of such influential students of narrative point of view as Wayne Booth and Boris Uspensky, but he is not at all interested in the formal properties of oral narrative texts. Indeed, he presents no texts at all in his discussion of personal experience narratives. He tells us, for instance, that

> A tale or anecdote, that is, a replaying, is not merely any reporting of a past event. In the fullest sense, it is such a statement couched from the personal perspective of an actual or potential participant who is located so that some temporal, dramatic development of the reported event proceeds from that starting point. (1974:504)

But how does this management of personal perspective operate in actual narratives? How does it govern the way that narratives are made, if it is indeed a significant factor in what they are about and how they work? Goffman does not address these issues.

My argument is this: If we are to develop our understanding of those stories we have labeled personal experience narratives, thereby implicating the relationship between narrative and event and the management of point of view, then it is crucial that we set about investigating those dimensions of relationship directly, bolstering our social and linguistic insights with literary ones, toward a deeper and more nuanced comprehension of the forms and functions of this powerful expressive vehicle. This chapter is offered as preliminary exploration in that direction.

Specifically, what I propose to examine in this chapter is a small corpus of first-person narratives about practical jokes. My reasons for focusing on stories of this kind are twofold. First, *both* the stories and the events they recount are of special interest to students of the interaction order, making the investigation of their interrelationship doubly productive. Goffman himself notes the special narrative potential of practical jokes (1959:12), and folklorist Richard Tallman (1974) goes so far as to suggest that practical jokes and stories about them are two complementary parts of the same expressive tradition (see also Cothran 1974:349), which may in fact be linked more broadly to the tall-tale tradition explored in Chapters 2 and 5 of this book. Second, in practical jokes access to and management of information are especially problematic. Practical jokes are built on complex structures of information management, involving dimensions of backstage activity, frame manipulation, fabrication, concealment, and differential access to information about what is going on. Accordingly, the problem of point of view takes on special interest in narratives about practical jokes. Essentially, how does one construct a story about a practical joke in which one has been involved?

The corpus of narratives I will examine consists of three stories, all told by the same man, representative of his repertoire of personal narratives about practical joking in which he had a central role. I will look primarily at texts of the stories recorded in 1983, but with occasional reference to earlier tellings of two of them, recorded in 1981.

The narrator is a native West Texan, now in his early eighties, whom I will call, pseudonymously, Merle Hannum. He has spent most of his life in a town of a little more than 5,000 in population, pursuing a variety of enterprises including operating a hardware store and a lumber yard, but he has also maintained an involvement in ranching throughout his adult life. Also throughout his adult life, he maintained particularly close relationships of friendship and sociability with a group of men (most of them now deceased) who drank coffee, fished, hunted, and played dominoes together. The social life of this circle included a strong joking component, manifested especially in verbal teasing and practical jokes: "There's about ten or twelve, fifteen of us has been that way all of our lives, just teasin' one another and playin' jokes on one another."

The participants were ever alert for opportunities to get one off on each other in a constant contest of wits. The tone of this expressive fool making within the group was always playful, but nevertheless competitive, a ludic exercise in dominance, control, and display (cf. Brandes 1980:116–28). And whether the joking was verbal or practical, it provided a ready supply of material for narratives which replayed the original experiences. For the winners of these joking contests, the stories provided a second expressive vehicle for performance, whereas for the victims, who also told stories recounting their own discomfiture, they represented an opportunity to display their storytelling abilities as well as to confirm their good sportsmanship. To be an accomplished joker, a good sport, and a good storyteller are all valued in this West Texas cattle culture, so one might also tell these stories on other occasions as well, such as family reunions.

Before proceeding to the stories, I must make clear what I mean by practical jokes. I consider practical jokes to be part of a large class of expressive routines of victimization, playful deceits that include put-ons, tall tales, catch routines, hoaxes, and so on (Goffman 1974:87–103; McDowell 1979:39–40; Philips 1975; Roemer 1977). It is not my purpose here to formulate a rigorous typology of such routines (cf. Goffman 1974; Tallman 1974). Rather, I wish simply to set out a working definition (influenced largely by Goffman 1974:89 and Esar 1952:184) that captures the kind of deceits that form the basis for these stories, all of which are covered locally by the phrase "playing jokes on one another." These are enactments of playful deceit in which one party or team (to be called *trickster*) intentionally manipulates features of a situation in such a way as to induce another person or persons (to be called *victim* or *dupe*) to have a false or misleading sense of what is going on and so to behave in a way that brings about discomfiture (confusion, embarrassment, etc.) in the victim. That is, practical jokes all involve fabrication in the sense developed by Goffman: "A nefarious design is involved, a plot or treacherous plan leading – when realized – to a falsification of some part of the world" (1974:83). Nevertheless, again to adopt Goffman's distinction, these are all benign fabrications, in which the victim's moral character or other serious interests (e.g., economic) do not suffer any real damage (1974:87).

Practical jokes of the kind I am concerned with differ from put-ons, kidding, and teasing in that they are relatively more elaborate and highly orchestrated fabrications and involve manipulation of the victim's immediate social and cognitive environment beyond the verbal, including objects, actions, other people, and social relations. This is what makes them *practical* jokes: They involve fabrication of part of the extraverbal world, though words may be among the means employed to effect the trickery. As engineered fabrications, crafted deceits, practical jokes involve by their very nature a differential access to and distribution of information about what is going on, with the trickster having a more "real" sense of the situation, while the victim has a "false" one. There may also be bystanders to the situation whose information states will vary depending on the extent to which they have been let in on the joke by the trickster and the extent of their knowledge of the features of the victim's informational environment that are being manipulated by the trickster.

The main problem I want to explore in what follows is how these differential information states are handled in the stories recounting practical jokes. Specifically, Mr. Hannum tells stories about practical jokes in which he was the trickster and others in which he was the dupe. Thus, although all are first-person narratives, as participant in the original events he had different kinds of knowledge about what was going on at various points in the enactment of the joke. As narrator, however, in his retrospective replaying of the events, he has a fuller knowledge of the events and their outcomes. How does he organize what he knew then and what he knows now in the construction of his stories? And a related question: How does he manage the audience's access to information about what is going on in the narrated event?

Let us consider first a story about a practical joke in which Mr. Hannum himself was the trickster.

Ketchup and Mustard (1983)

But the funniest one that I ever pulled is, I had a place out there on the creek where we went fishing. You know, a bunch of us'd go out, catch a bunch of fish and fry 'em an' stay there till ten, eleven o'clock or twelve, playin' dominoes.

So one night, I always had to do all the cookin', they cleaned the fish an' I'd cook 'em. Well, while I was cookin' those fish, I mixed up a bunch o' ketchup and a bunch o' mustard, all mixed it up together and put it out on the long porch.

And we got to playin' dominoes purty good, and I grabbed my stomach and made like I was . . . had a cramp and had to . . . I hollered "I've gotta go t'the bushes," or somethin', you know, and . . . and course all of 'em went to hollerin' at me 'bout something, you know. "Kill it before you get back," or stuff like that, you know.

So, I come back in – I just went on the outside and I had this roll o' toilet paper out there too, y'see, and I just took that toilet paper and wiped up that mustard and ketchup mixed up together, and it looked like the real stuff, see?

I come in there and this boy's settin' there playin' 'is dominoes, y'know, and 'is hand like this [gestures], I says, "You wanted me to bring some of it back, here it is.'' So I just dropped it over on 'is hands.

He . . . he got up and says, ''Ohhh, Merle, I wouldn't do nobody that way,'' and he got up and walked over t'the basin and nose all turned up, just about to vomit, washed 'is hands real good, and got 'im a rag and come back, cleared off 'is table, and the paper was still layin' there right on it, you know, and I just walked over there and raked my finger through it [tastes it], I said, ''Why, Alvin, that's not bad.''

He . . . he never did forgive me for that. He . . . he swore that he could smell it, and he said, ''Why, man, I could smell it,'' he says, ''it was just terrible.''

In this story, the narrator himself was the trickster, or rather – since we will want to distinguish between the information states of the narrator and the trickster – the story is narrated by the person who had the role of trickster in the original enactment. His role is made explicit in the opening line. Our preceding conversation dealt with practical joking in general and within his circle of friends, and he now introduces his account of a specific joke as ''the funniest one I ever pulled.'' Thus, as trickster, he was in the most privileged position of all in the enactment (Booth 1983:160–3; Doložel 1980:18); as the one who orchestrated the fabrication and pulled it off, he had the clearest idea of what was going on throughout the encounter.

As narrator, recounting past experience, Mr. Hannum is also in the most privileged position in the storytelling event: He knows how it will turn out, whereas we the audience do not – at least the first time we hear the story.

After introducing the story as dealing with ''the funniest one I ever pulled,'' the narrator offers certain background information by way of orientation (Labov and Waletzky 1967:32), the external conditions and factors that brought the participants into place and provided the means for the subsequent trick: A group of men has gathered out at Mr. Hannum's place on the creek to fish, eat, and play dominoes. This is the sociable group of jokers alluded to earlier, gathered together for an occasion of play (fishing and dominoes) in a place physically set apart from the town and used primarily for such play activities. All conditions are thus highly conducive to joking activity.

The first particle, ''so,'' as so often in Anglo-American storytelling, signals the transition from orientation – background and potentiating conditions – to the actual time line of the story. Here is where point of view and the management of information first become problematic. The narrator tells us that ''while I was cookin' those fish, I mixed up a bunch o' ketchup and a bunch o' mustard, all mixed it up together and put it out on the long porch.'' This is apparently part of the setup for the practical joke – the mixture is a strange one and evidently not part of the food to be eaten. The action takes place backstage (Goffman 1959:112), out of sight of the others and before the actual enactment, but we as audience are permitted through Hannum's verbal account to witness this act of preparation. In effect, the narrator takes us backstage and lets us in on his preparations for the trick. This is information he would be privy to, as he is recounting his own past actions. All that we are shown, however, is his outward behavior, the preparation of the mixture and the placing of it on the porch. We are not told what his plan is, why the mixture is prepared, what it will be used for, what kind of joke is developing, and so on. Thus, an element of suspense is introduced into the narrative, as the audience is presented with a bit of curious information, but a full explanation of its implications is withheld (cf. Goffman 1974:506–8).

The story then skips ahead to what the narrator considers the next relevant scene, omitting intervening actions such as eating, initiating the game of dominoes, and so on, and proceeding to the point where "we got to playin' dominoes purty good." This turns out to be the episode in which the fabrication is actually enacted, the pulling of the joke itself. The element of fabrication is clearly and explicitly indicated by the phrase "made like"; the apparent action is a pretense, to give the impression that the trickster has a cramp and has to go out to relieve himself. This part of the fabrication is made up of the physical action of grabbing his stomach as if he had a cramp plus the verbal statement of the need to go outside.

The other players all fall for the fabrication and go into what is apparently a standard joking routine for them under such circumstances, giving the departing member outrageous instructions about the disposition of his feces, such as "kill it before you get back." The conventional nature of such routines is indicated by the phrases *"course* all of 'em went to hollerin' "* and "stuff like that." This underscores the ambience of licensed joking that existed within the group and in this setting; scatological joking is a playful contravention of the usual taboo against talking about elimination and its products.

Where does this bring us with regard to the management of information concerning what is going on? The overt action taking place in this scene is all out on the frontstage (Goffman 1959:107), visible to all. However, we as audience are given a key piece of information to which the others in the original situation are not privy, namely, the fact that the cramp is feigned, it is a fabrication. As before, though, we are not told explicitly why the action was done in terms of its ultimate purpose in the practical joke. But we can infer at this point that the resultant ragging by the other players was the immediate reaction aimed at by the trickster, what he hoped to elicit, with a confidence based on the routinized nature of kidding within the group. In other words, part of the setup for the joke, part of the resources mobilized by the trickster in its enactment, was the expectation that the others would react in this predictable way to a particular action on his part. The fabrication was designed to elicit this reaction, and the others are playing into his hands. When they respond as expected, the implication is that they are contributing to their own victimization. Also, we are prompted to speculate about the possible connections between this fabrication on the part of the trickster and his earlier backstage preparation of the ketchup and mustard mixture. The connection between this messy concoction and feces is available to be made.

Thus, at this stage, we as audience remain informationally somewhere between the trickster and the victims. He knows exactly what he is up to and what he expects to follow, whereas the victims have only a false sense of what is going on immediately before them. We know, because the narrator has let us in on it, that a fabrication is in progress that has involved some prior backstage preparation and a current feigned action, and we have an emerging inkling of what will follow – that someone is to be victimized and that the prepared mixture and the players' response to the feigned cramp will figure in it.

It is useful to consider these differential information states (Genette 1980:206) in terms of the interplay of time, action, and comprehension. The trickster has a clear view of what he has done prior to this scene, what he is doing in this scene, and what he expects to follow. The victim has only a false view of what is going on in the immediate scene. The audience has a view of what has happened earlier backstage but only an emerging sense of why; a view of what is going on in the immediate scene that we know is a fabrication but again only an emerging sense why; and a tentative sense of what will follow – that it will lead to victimization and that the means we have seen coming together (the mustard–ketchup mixture, the other player's belief that Mr. Hannum is going out to relieve himself, and their kidding routines) will somehow work to produce that effect. What added insight we as audience have into the emerging practical joke beyond that of the other participants is controlled by the narrator, who lets us see himself as trickster, but does not tell us what he intends. The suspense continues.

In the next episode, the connection between the earlier preparations and the feigned cramp becomes clear. Once again, we are allowed backstage with the trickster as he wipes up some of the ketchup–mustard mixture with toilet paper and reveals its purpose: It was fabricated to pass for feces – "it looked like the real stuff."

Securing the mess sets up the culmination of the joke itself, the springing of the trap in which the victimization of the dupe is accomplished. The trickster returns to the group and drops the toilet tissue with the mixture on it on the hands of one of the players, publicly rationalizing this act of defilement (cf. Goffman 1971:46–9) by appeal to the earlier kidding directed at him by the group as he left to go outside. Apparently, though he did not say so earlier, one of the cracks directed at him as part of the kidding routine was "bring some back." Offered in jest, this comment was hardly meant to be taken seriously and no competent member of the group should have done so, but here the trickster makes it appear – more fabrication – that that is in fact what he has done, or at best that he is himself carrying the kidding a bit further but in very bad taste. There is a nice reflexive touch here, in Mr. Hannum's subversive exploitation of the joking frame established earlier by the others, including the victim, in order to pull off a practical joke of his own. For this group, this kind of turning of the tables distinguishes a masterful practical joke and makes it especially reportable.

At this point of the story, we as hearers have fully caught up informationally with the trickster at the corresponding point of the enactment itself: We know why he has undertaken his various preparatory actions and how the victimization is to be effected. With the trickster, we can now observe the full discomfiture of the dupe.

And fully discomfited he is. He is completely taken in by the fabrication, taking the ketchup and mustard for "the real stuff," and he is appalled and revolted by this defilement visited upon him. In his view, the playful frame of the occasion has been shattered; the act of defilement exceeds all bounds of acceptability. He might make scatalogical jokes when a man goes off to relieve himself, but he "wouldn't do nobody" the way he thinks he has been done.

After allowing the victim to endure his discomfiture for a brief while, wash his hands, and clean the table, the trickster brings the joke to a close. What happens is that the trickster ultimately discredits his own fabrication (Goffman 1974:84–5) by working a reverse bit of impression management on the dupe. Playing upon Alvin's mistaken understanding that the ketchup and mustard are the real stuff, the trickster administers another shock to him by undermining *that* understanding by putting some of the mixture in his mouth. Although the narrator does not describe the effect of this discrediting action, we can almost see the whole fabricational frame fall apart as Alvin catches on to what is going on and to how fully he has been manipulated by Mr. Hannum.

The trick now over, it remains only to wind up the story. The statement, "He never did forgive me for that" conveys two bits of information, both testimonials to the efficacy of the joke. First there is the claim that the effect of the joke was so strong and its success so complete that it was unforgettable. It is not that Alvin really never did forgive Mr. Hannum, but rather the suggestion is that he continued to concede how drastically taken in and discomfited he was whenever the joke was recounted or alluded to thereafter. And this is the second key point – that the group did talk about this joke repeatedly after it was enacted. The final statement about the smell is a kind of evaluative coda (cf. Labov and Waletzky 1967:33–40), underscoring yet again the efficacy of the central fabrication to drive home the reportability of the event.

Let us turn now to our second story, in which the narrator again played the role of trickster in the event being recounted.

The Theft of the Watermelon (1983)

That happened here in . . . in uh . . . while I was runnin' the hardware store. This is what happened this friend o' mine brought me a great big watermelon, a nice one, and . . . and I had a coupla friends run the fillin' station right behind me, you see, and uh, they slipped up there and stole the watermelon.

So they hid it, you know. They's gonna just make me hunt for it.

Well, I knew they got it, right as soon as I missed it I knew who got it, so I got out there in town and . . . and, uh, found a man that was kinda radical, you know, and high-tempered, and a friend o' mine too, since we lived out there on the farm, and I got him to come by the store after his watermelon, see?

And one o' these boys'd been watchin' me all day to see when I'd miss it. So I got this man t'come in and t'ask me where 'is watermelon was, and I says, "Oh, I guess it's still out there where it was, it's under some tables," and we went back and looked and it was gone.

I says, "No, it's gone, I don' know who's got it, or where it's at," and I says, "Are you sure it was left here?"

He says, "Yeah, it was so-and-so told me he left it here for me."

And . . . and so, we couldn't find the watermelon and he just throwed a fit and cussed me out and all about gettin' 'is watermelon. Course we had it all planned, y'see? And so he just got in 'is car and tol' me, says, "I'll never come back in this place again to buy anything," and just left just mad as a wet hen, see?

Well, one o' those boys was settin' in there at that time. Of course, he heard it all and saw it all and I noticed he got up and sneaked out the back. And uh, didn't say nothin'.

That man hadn't any more'n got home till they loaded that watermelon up in their car, took it out to 'im. Tol' 'im, says, "We thought it was Merle's watermelon," says, "we didn't know it was yours," says, "we wouldn'a got it at all," and 'pologized for it and told 'im that I wasn't responsible, not to hold me responsible, that I didn't have nothin' t'do with it, and uh, so, uh . . . after they got through 'pologizin', why, he asked 'em in and they cut it and he told 'em about it.

That was kinda funny how we turned the joke on 'em.

This story begins, after a minimal orientational sentence, with a brief account of a prank played on Mr. Hannum by other members of his joking group. Two friends who ran the filling station behind his store, and were thus in a position to see what went on there, playfully stole and hid a gift watermelon to provoke a reaction from Mr. Hannum as his expectations concerning its whereabouts were undermined. That is, they attempted a practical joke on him, and he is recounting something he did not witness, backstage activities at which he was not present. At this early point, then, by contrast with the other story, Mr. Hannum's story persona is informationally behind himself as narrator concerning what was going on around him. He is also behind the tricksters. We as audience are privy to information that Mr. Hannum did not have at that stage of the original event narrated in the opening lines of the story.

He catches up quickly, though, and the trick fails as he guesses immediately what is going on. Having caught on to the attempted trick, he proceeds to go on the offensive with one of his own, using his friends' setup and their sense of his sense of what is going on as resources for the joke that will turn the tables on them.

But note that the story does not tell us all this as yet. Rather, as in the ketchup and mustard story, the narrative proceeds to an account of action that is part of Mr. Hannum's own backstage setup but again, as in the earlier story, without an explanation of why exactly he is undertaking this action, what it is intended to produce. Hannum's own setup involves the recruitment of another person to collude with him in his fabrication, and the planning of the fabrication itself. They will put on a little act to give the false impression that the melon belongs not to Hannum but to his farmer accomplice who is well cast for the part, being known for his high temper and "radical" (i.e., quick-to-anger) manner. The account of the setup includes attention to potentiating conditions: The thief is sitting around waiting for Mr. Hannum to miss his watermelon, in the false belief that Hannum doesn't know what is going on. The earlier account of the friends stealing the melon has now become orientational background for Mr. Hannum's own trick, setting out the factors that bring people into place for its enactment and provide the means for pulling it off. Thus, although the narrator does not tell us exactly why his narrated persona is arranging things in this way, and the purpose of the fabrication is more readily intuited than the mixing of the ketchup and mustard, this story is now on a track parallel to the earlier one: It begins with orientational background and proceeds to an account of the backstage setup of the central practical joke to which we as audience are privy while the intended victim is not.

The structural correspondence continues with the next segment of the story, which, as before, is the enactment of the trick itself, the duping of the victim. To this end, the trickster and his accomplice enact a little skit in which the farmer asks for the melon as if it were his, Mr. Hannum looks for it as if he really expected to find it, and the farmer responds with angry words as if he were really mad. These actions are explicitly identified as feigned: "I got this man t'come in and t'ask me where 'is watermelon was," and "Course we had it all planned, y'see?" I would suggest, though, that their feigned nature is clear enough without being made explicit. It is interesting to note that the actual description of action in this little staged scene is expressed in terms of what is visible on the surface: not ''he *pretended* to throw a fit,'' but simply ''he just throwed a fit.''

The fabrication now enacted, the narrative shifts to the reaction of the dupe. He gets up, leaves the store, gets his own accomplice and the watermelon, and they proceed to drive it out to the farmer's house. They have been taken in by the fabrication. Here again, there is a nice reflexive element in their victimization: In terms of their understanding of what is going on, it is their own sense of the limits of acceptable joking that makes them susceptible to Mr. Hannum's countertrick and proves their undoing. It is all right to spirit off a melon that belongs to another member of the joking group, but things have gone too far when the melon actually belongs to someone else, Hannum is angrily blamed for stealing it, and his reputation and business might be threatened by this act of which he is innocent. Thus, the dupes experience the discomfiture of having gone too far and of violating their own moral sense and attempt to make amends by returning the melon to the person they now assume is its rightful owner, thereby exonerating Mr. Hannum.

Once they have expressed their contrition and displayed their embarrassment, the farmer, like Hannum himself in the preceding story, discredits the fabrication in which he has himself participated by telling them what has actually been going on. Finally, this story, again like the earlier one, closes with an evaluation: ''That was kinda funny how we turned the joke on 'em.''

A crucial point, however: Note that from the point at which the melon thief leaves the store, the events recounted in the narrative occurred out of Hannum's view. This is not necessarily uncommon in practical jokes, in which the trickster manipulates things in order to induce the victim to have a false sense of what is going on but in which the consequences of that sense may be deferred. But our concern here is with the implications for the *story* of this separation of the narrative action from Mr. Hannum's first person narrative persona. In terms of the narrative, Hannum the narrator separates himself from Hannum the trickster, and, taking the audience with him, follows the action to its end by following the victims as they experience their discomfiture and embarrassment and are eventually told that they have been had. In order to do this, Hannum the narrator gives the hearers information that he could have gained only sometime afterward as the participants recounted and re-played the trick.

It is interesting to note in this connection that even though he was not present during the confrontation between the melon thieves and the farmer, he reports part of the interaction in direct discourse, verbally showing the audience a scene that he himself did not witness. In the ketchup and mustard story, we might expect direct quotation, as the narrator was an eyewitness to the events he is recounting. It turns out that the direct discourse is a fictional device on both occasions (cf. Sternberg 1982), for in other tellings of the same story that I have recorded the quoted passages are different. In the watermelon story, however, the reported speech is at a double remove, for he is reporting speech that was subsequently reported to him by the participants. I will deal further with this later in the chapter. For now, let us take stock of what we have learned thus far about the construction of Mr. Hannum's stories about practical jokes.

We may begin by noting that both stories we have examined have closely similar structures, proceeding from an initial presentation of background information to set the stage, to the setup of the practical joke, to the actual trick event, to the discrediting of the fabrication on which the joke turns, to a final evaluation of the joke. The structure may be outlined thus:

I. *Orientation.* This section sets out the factors that bring the participants into place for the practical joke to be recounted and that provide the means (e.g., objects, patterns of social relations, interactional routines) for enacting it.

II. *Setup.* Here is recounted the engineering of the trick, the mobilization of the means to set up the fabrication on which the joke will turn. This portion of the narrative includes consideration and exploitation of the potentiating conditions for the joke: the character of key participants, the nature of the situation, habitual orientations, expectations, routines, and so on. The setup takes place in a backstage sphere, out of sight of the intended victim and other bystanders who are not in collusion with the trickster.

III. *Trick event.* The stories then proceed to a recounting of the actual working of the key fabrication on the dupe. Here the action shifts to frontstage, although part of it may be outside the view of the trickster and may be interspersed with further backstage activity. The trick event episode consists of the following sequence of actions:

A. Enactment of the fabrication, in which the dupe is induced to have a false or misleading sense of what is going on

B. Effect of the fabrication on the victim
1. Emotional effects, such as embarrassment, confusion, guilt, and loss of face
2. Victim's reaction, that is, what the victim does in reaction to the enactment and its emotional effects

IV. *Discrediting of the fabrication.* After the victim endures his discomfiture for a while, the fabrication frame is broken and the working of the joke is revealed.

V. *Evaluation.* The stories close with an evaluative comment concerning the efficacy of the practical joke.

Insofar as it is part of the essence of narrative to recount an event, to tell about some sequence of actions that happened, sections II–IV *(Setup, Trick event,* and *Discrediting)* constitute the core of Mr. Hannum's practical joke stories.[1] I would suggest that the narrative development of these sections mirrors Hannum's understanding of the functional stages of a practical joke that need to be covered in an adequate narrative account.

In the first story, about the ketchup and mustard, the narrator remains quite closely merged with his narrative persona as trickster in the narrated event. The trickster was present through all the above-listed functional stages, so the narration can be accomplished by following him around, so to speak, as he moves from backstage preparation to the frontstage scene of the first part of his fabrication (the feigning of a cramp), back to the backstage securing of the ketchup–mustard mixture, to the frontstage feigned defilement of the dupe. Essentially, what is recounted to us in the narrative is what we might have seen or heard had we been there beside the trickster in the narrated event. This latter statement must be qualified by acknowledging the creative license accorded the narrator, as, for example, in his use of quoted speech, which varies from one recounting of the story to the next. The one thing we could not have known from direct observation is that the act he is pulling off in grabbing his stomach before the victim is a fabrication, and this the narrator reveals to us verbally in the story. And, as we have noted, some suspense is maintained with regard to *why* the trickster is doing what he does, how he envisions that the trick will play itself out. Still, knowing that some of his actions are fabrications and having a view of what goes on backstage allows us to catch on to what is going on before the victim and the bystanders can do so.

In the watermelon story, Mr. Hannum is again the trickster and the narrative follows the same structure, but Hannum was not present during the unfolding of the full functional sequence as he was in the first story. He did not witness the theft of the watermelon that becomes part of the potentiating conditions of his own trick, and he did not witness any of the actions that took place after the thief left his store. In telling the story, then, the narrator takes us along the sequence of functional stages of the practical joke, whether he was directly involved or not, splitting off from his narrated persona when necessary. Again, we get to see what goes on backstage, and we are told when a particular act by the trickster is a fabrication, but the narrator tells us nothing about what specifically the trickster hoped to accomplish by the fabrication – that we must figure out for ourselves as the story unfolds. Here too, then, some narrative suspense is maintained, but we are still enabled by the information that the narrator provides to catch on to the working and effects of the trick at a point in the story corresponding to a point in the narrated event before the fabrication is discredited.

---

[1]   It is illuminating to compare the structure of these narratives about practical jokes to those of trickster tales (Galin 1981) and swindler tales (Jason 1971). All are about fabrication, with the result that they share suggestive similarities of structure; this merits further investigation.

Thus far, we have confirmed our examination to stories told by Mr. Hannum about practical jokes in which he was the trickster. But these are not the only kind of practical joke narratives that he tells. Like the dog traders who tell stories about trades in which they have been taken because they appreciate the trading game for its own sake and the opportunity for performance that the stories provide, Mr. Hannum tells about practical jokes in which he was the victim. In his sociable group of jokers, what counts is the cleverness and effectiveness of the trick and the expressive opportunity afforded by telling about it. Here is one of his stories about his own victimization, from the same storytelling session as the other two.

The Thwarted Horse Sale (1983)

Yeah, there's a man out here in the country, a farmer, horse died. He come to town lookin' for a horse, and he was a radical kind of a guy, and . . . and wasn't very smart – he wasn't any smarter'n I am, I don't guess – anyway, he struck some friends o' mine there on the town . . . on the street, and says, "Where could I find a good horse?"

And this ol' boy says, "Merle Hannum has got one for sale." Says, "He'll tell you that he don't wanna sell it, but he's just tellin' you that just to where you'd . . . you'd pay a high price for it." And he says, "You'll have to tell him . . . he'll try to tell you that he don' wanna sell it."

And that ol' boy come up there and he hit me up for that horse. Wanteda know if I had a horse for sale.

I said, "No, I sure haven't, Clark."

He says, "Well, some very responsible friends of yours told me you had a horse for sale," and he says, "I need a horse bad." He says, "I wanna buy that horse."

I says, "Well, Clark, I don' have no horse."

And he says, "I know damn well you have," he says. "They told me you'd tell me that just to get a high price." Says, "just tell me how much you want for 'im."

And I said, "Clark, I don't have a horse."

But he . . . he just wouldn't believe it, see?

And . . . and then I looked across the street over there and them boys'd follered 'im up, just standin' 'cross the street, just dyin' laughin'. I didn't even have a horse – they just told 'im that, see? An' he was about to whip me 'cause I wouldn't sell 'im a horse. He says I'd just as soon . . . "You'd just as well let me have that horse as anybody," says, "I want that horse."

He like to whipped me over it.

The first thing we may observe about this narrative is that it follows the same structural pattern as those we have already examined.

I. *Orientation.* The farmer comes to town in search of a horse to replace
    one of his animals that has died. He is described as high-tempered
    and not very smart, both qualities that help make the subsequent
    practical joke possible and that will be exploited by the trickster. He
    encounters the tricksters on the street and the trick can be set in
    motion.

II. *Setup.* The friends set up the fabrication by telling the farmer that Han-
    num has a horse but will act as if he doesn't want to sell it in order
    to drive up the price. In this, they are taking advantage of the farm-
    er's need and credulity. Here, as in the other stories, there is a clever
    reflexive turn, insofar as their fabrication is built upon the imputation
    of a fabrication to Hannum; the false sense of what is going on that
    they induce in the farmer is that *Hannum* will attempt to induce a
    false sense of what is going on in him.

    Note that the encounter of the farmer with Hannum's friends that
    leads to the setup of the practical joke takes place out of Hannum's
    view. From his perspective, the setup is backstage; he does not enter
    the joke sequence until later. Here again, then, Hannum the narrator
    is separate from Hannum the participant in the narrated action. From
    the standpoint of the narrative, he is more the omniscient narrator at
    the opening of the story than the reporter of personal experience,
    presenting information he acquired subsequent to the event but that
    must be presented here in order to follow what is for him the proper
    constructional sequence for a practical joke story. As before, his use
    of quoted speech in reporting this encounter at which he was not
    himself present is a fictive report of a report of what was said.

III. *Trick event.* Here it must be noted that in objective terms there are really
    two victims of this joke. Both Hannum and the farmer are manipu-
    lated into a state of confusing, conflictful, and disjunctive interaction
    centering on the latter's attempt to purchase a horse that the former
    does not have, and each experiences the discomfiture of not being
    able to square his understanding of what is going on with the actions
    of the other (cf. Brandes 1980:121). But on the basis of the intense
    set of the group of jokers toward pulling off jokes on members of the
    joking circle – of which Mr. Hannum is a member and the farmer is
    not – one might consider that the tricksters targeted their joking ef-
    fort primarily at Mr. Hannum, using the farmer as a means toward
    that end, especially well-suited for the purpose because his "radical"
    nature would intensify the disjunction in his interaction with Han-
    num. In any event, it is clear that Hannum, the narrator of the story,
    views himself as the primary target.

IV. *Discrediting of the fabrication.* Note in support of the above suggestion
    that the routine is discredited when *Hannum* sees *his* friends across

the street "just dyin' laughin' "; there is no mention of the farmer here and how the joke is discredited for him.

V. *Evaluation.* Hannum's closing statement, "He like to whipped me over it," is a comment on the efficacy of the joke, underscoring how intense the conflictful interaction set up by the tricksters had become, very nearly reaching a point at which Hannum might have been seriously victimized indeed.

We have established, then, that Mr. Hannum's practical joke stories follow the same structural sequence whether he was trickster or victim in the original event. One significant consequence of this is that Hannum the narrator will separate himself narratively from Hannum the participant at those points in the proper sequence for recounting the practical joke for which he was not present at the action. At this point we may ask whether the difference in his participatory role – trickster versus victim – has any effect on the organization and presentation and the management of point of view in the respective stories.

When Hannum recounts the jokes he has pulled himself, we have observed that he does so for the most part without revealing why he is doing a particular action, what effects he is aiming for, thereby preserving a degree of narrative suspense, but that he *does* tell us when he is engaged in fabrication. In this story about the thwarted horse sale, however, even though Hannum knows that the information given to the farmer about his having a horse and being reluctant to sell it is a fabrication, he says nothing in the story about its being so.

The context of the storytelling session, devoted as it is to stories about practical jokes, lets us know that what we are hearing about has a fabrication in it somewhere, but in terms of the story itself, the whole sequence of setup and trick event is presented in terms of overt action, all of which might be "straight." That is, for all we are told, what Hannum's friends tell the farmer might well be true, and Hannum's behavior in the trick event would confirm it. We might guess that he doesn't have the horse, because that is a likely point for the fabrication to turn on and we are developing an intuitive sense ourselves of the structure of the stories and where the consequences of the fabrication are played out, but it is not until after he recounts the discrediting experience of seeing his friends laughing that the narrator makes the essence of the fabrication explicit in the story: "I didn't even have a horse – they just told 'im that, see?"

In these terms, then, it does make some difference whether Hannum was trickster or victim. When the former, he tells us what is fabrication, presumably because he was the one who engineered it and would know about it; when the latter, he does not tell us what is fabrication, because that is information to which he as participant in the narrated event was not privy, the

mental states of the other narrative agents being inaccessible to him (cf. Doložel 1980:18). That is, although he does use his retrospective and compre-
hensive knowledge as narrator to present information that his narrative persona could not know at a particular point in the unfolding of the original
event, when it is required by the narrative structure he follows in recounting
practical jokes, he does not do so in order to reveal a fabrication that was not
of his doing.

The various findings we have presented have some significant implications
for our understanding of "personal experience narratives," the matter on which
we opened this chapter. Mr. Hannum's structuring of his narratives about
practical jokes indicates that for him the phase structure (Turner 1974:36) of
the practical joking; that is, the practical joke as a coherent processual event
is the guiding principle in the making of a story. In the first story we examined, about the ketchup and mustard, the narrative follows the setup–trick
event–discrediting sequence quite clearly, with this core of the narrative framed
by the opening orientation (to mobilize the resources for the joke) and the
closing evaluation (to comment on the efficacy of the trick). The orientation
and evaluation sections are special features of the narrative recounting of the
event; they are not themselves part of the representation of the sequence
of actions making up the practical joke event, although they – especially
the orientation – perform an essential function in communicating effectively
about the event. The orientation and evaluation help establish and convey a
sense of the boundaries of the event, its separability from the surrounding
flow of action and experience in a way that makes cognitive and communicative
sense.

The fact that the narrative core of this first story follows the phase structure
of the practical joke is not surprising, because this structure coincides so completely with Hannum's actions and experience within the event. It appears
quite natural for the account to follow the event structure because everything
reported on was accessible to the narrator's knowledge or observation as a
participant. This is, then, fully a narrative of personal experience, albeit of
personal experience within a larger social context in which others figured as
well.

When we come to the remaining two stories, however, about the theft of
the watermelon and the horse sale, other factors are at work. In both stories,
as we have seen, the core of the narrative again follows the phase structure
of the practical joke: setup, enactment, discrediting. But in both, parts of the
overall event, defined in terms of the functional stages of the practical joke,
were not immediately accessible to Hannum as participant. In the watermelon
trick, the theft of the melon and the crucial discomfiture of the victims and
the discrediting of the joke took place in his absence. In the horse sale, the
setup was accomplished out of his sight, quite appropriately and necessarily,
as he was the intended dupe, the one to be contained by the fabrication.

Hannum does not begin this story, or the one about the watermelon, at the point at which he enters the action or terminate at the point where he leaves the action.

In these terms, then, the two stories are not fully narratives of personal experience, despite the fact that Hannum considers himself centrally implicated in both, once as trickster, once as dupe. Rather, here the personal involvement of the narrator as protagonist is subordinate to the structure of the event; it is the phase structure of the event that gives structure to the narratives, not the personal involvement of the narrator in the original action. In telling the stories, Hannum the narrator departs from his own immediate involvement in the narrated action where necessary to recount the full event in the proper sequence of its functional stages. In order to do so, he must draw upon information for the narratives that he could not have acquired until after the fact. I will return to this point shortly.

These considerations raise a point of considerable significance in narrative theory, namely, in what way events may be taken to be prior to and determinative of the narratives that recount them and in what way the events may be seen as being retroactively *constituted* by the narratives. I have discussed the general issues surrounding this problem in the introduction to this book and will not repeat them here. Rather, I will ask what light is shed on the problem by the practical joke narratives at hand.

I would argue that in the stories we have examined, the event is in an important sense antecedent to and determinative of the narratives in structural terms. Practical joke events, especially for seasoned practical jokers like Mr. Hannum and his friends, do not need to be constituted by the narratives about them, for they have a known structure of their own, understood, anticipated, and planned for from the beginning in the pulling off of a practical joke. Practical jokes like those recounted in these stories are crafted routines, constructed and managed just as stories are. Pulling a practical joke is a conscious act; to carry one off requires that the structure be in some sense – tacitly, if not fully consciously – objectified and known by the perpetrator. For any given story, then, the general event structure of practical jokes is already well known, and its internal sequence of functional stages is what must be followed, in Hannum's conception, in constructing the story.

Notwithstanding the priority of the event structure in the construction of the narratives, however, it is true that for Mr. Hannum and his friends stories help to objectify this event structure and make it known. I believe that hearing and telling stories about practical jokes was part of the process for these men of becoming a seasoned, skillful joker; by recounting and evaluating the jokes in narrative form, one clarifies how practical jokes work and what makes them effective. Thus, whereas for each of Mr. Hannum's stories the event structure is independent of and antecedent to the narrative, in a general sense the compound knowledge gained by *both* doing and telling helps give shape to each new joke. In this sense, the stories in general contribute proactively to the constitution of new practical jokes.

I have spoken thus far in structural terms, dealing with the shaping effect of the phase structure of the practical jokes on the stories about them. On the level of specific content, though, there is an important sense in which stories may be said to be constitutive of the events they recount. We recall that in order to develop his stories in accordance with his conception of the structure of practical joke events, in two of them Mr. Hannum had to draw in information that was not available to him at the corresponding stage of the original event. This information he acquired through subsequent discussions with other participants, either immediately after the discrediting of the trick or during still later sessions of sociable interaction with those other participants, or both. I have no recordings of these sessions, but it is clear from Hannum's testimony that a substantial part of the information concerning the missing pieces of the event came to him in narrative form, as each participant replayed his own involvement in the joke just past.

These debriefing narratives, then, filled in the gaps in Hannum's own knowledge of the event, and in so doing we might justifiably say that they were at least partially constitutive of the joke event for him. They provide him with the specific content to fill out the event structure in terms of which he already operates in the making of both practical jokes and narratives about them. For present purposes, what is important is that they provide him with part of the means he needs to tell the stories in cases where he was not himself present at every stage of the event. In other words, we might say that it is not Hannum's story of the thwarted horse sale that is constitutive of the event, but the stories of others that help constitute the full event for him by fitting content to his knowledge of the structure and letting him know how the structure has been realized.

We arrive, then, for this small corpus of narratives, at a rather complex picture of the relationship between the narratives and the events they recount. In our exploration of the relationship, we have had to consider a full range of factors, intrinsic and extrinsic to the narratives themselves, including local social and individual conceptions of the event being recounted (routinized, objectified, with a known and understood structure), dimensions of the narrator's personal involvement in the original events, the structure of the narrative plots, the management of information and point of view in the narratives, other narratives about aspects of the same events, and so on. The relationship between story and event in these narratives thus turns out to be reciprocal, not in some vague, general, ineffable sense (cf. Culler 1981:186 –7) but in ways that can be demonstrated on the levels of content and structure.[2]

[2]   Sam Schrager comes to similar conclusions in his insightful article, ''What Is Social in Oral History?'' (1983).

I must emphasize, however, that we have examined in this exploration only three narratives told by one narrator and, although they are representative of his repertoire of practical joke stories, I can make no claim about the other first-person narratives he tells, about practical joke narratives told by others, or about first-person narratives in general. My purpose has been to demonstrate that the personal component of oral "personal experience narratives" (so-called) is more problematic than it has been considered and that a close literary and functional analysis of such first-person oral narratives can tell us much of interest about how they are made and about how they relate to the events they recount. Such processes and relationships are to be discovered, not assumed a priori or generalized from written literature.

4

"HELL, YES, BUT NOT THAT YOUNG"

Reported speech as comic corrective

Of all the devices by which the fusion of narrated event and narrative event is effected in narrative discourse, reported speech is perhaps the most sociolinguistically interesting. The appropriation of another's utterance, to be sure, is not confined to narrative contexts. As Bakhtin argues, "The transmission and assessment of the speech of others, the discourse of another, is one of the most widespread and fundamental topics of human speech. In all areas of life and ideological activity, our speech is filled to overflowing with other people's words" (1981:337). But Bakhtin himself has explored the patterns and functions of reported speech most fully in the novel, and other sociologists of language are finding it increasingly useful to examine the dynamics of speech actions and reactions in a variety of narrative forms, from oral stories of personal experience to myths, as a means of elucidating relations of speech, action, and ideology in the social worlds reported by such narratives (Labov 1982; Silverstein 1985; Urban 1984). There is a dual payoff here that is especially attractive to a language-oriented student of verbal art: Insofar as acts of speaking are of focal interest in certain kinds of narrative, an understanding of the ways that these speech acts are contextualized within the narrative can enhance our understanding both of how speaking operates and is understood to operate in social life *and* of how narratives are constructed.

Analysis of the use of reported speech in the foregoing discussion of stories about practical jokes helped to reveal the complex dynamics linking the joking routines themselves to the narratives that recount them and to the narrator's role in both. Here, I wish to bring reported speech to the center of attention, through a close examination of narratives that themselves center on reported speech.

I propose to examine in this chapter a small corpus of oral narratives I have recorded in which quoted speech is not only an artistic device but the very focus of the story; the reported speech is the maximally reportable act recounted in the narrative (Labov 1982). These stories represent forms of discourse in which the concern with and use of other people's words takes on a special heightened quality, in which these words become especially prominently the "object of interpretation, discussion, evaluation, rebuttal, support, further development and so on" of which Bakhtin writes (1981:337).

In generic terms, the narratives I will examine are anecdotes (Bødker 1965:26, 102–3; Botkin 1949; Röhrich 1977:6–8; Taylor 1970), one of the least studied of oral narrative forms. The anecdote may be defined as a short, humorous narrative, purporting to recount a true incident involving real people. The characteristic formal features of the genre include a focus on a single episode and a single scene, and a tendency to limit attention to two principal actors. As a corollary, perhaps, of this last feature, anecdotes also tend to be heavily dialogic in construction, often culminating in a kind of punch line, a striking, especially reportable statement rendered in direct discourse. That is to say, quoted speech is a significant stylistic feature of the genre (see, e.g., Carey 1976:85; Dorson 1964:65); accordingly, the anecdote would seem to offer itself as an apt focus for investigation of the formal and functional role of reported speech in oral narrative and of the interrelationships linking narrated event, narrative, and storytelling event.

The stories under study were all recorded from a single individual, a West Texas rancher, now in his early eighties. I will call him Caswell Rogers. Several types of anecdotes centering on reported speech have a place in Mr. Rogers's repertoire. One of his favorites, for example, involves a situation wherein he was traveling around the county raising support for a program of brush control and in which he was misunderstood – with very amusing consequences – by a very proper but slightly deaf old lady to be asking her to contribute for *birth* control.[1] Another favorite revolves around a complex insurance scam in which a man faked his own death and a funeral was held. Several years later, after he had returned to the community, he really died, and one man remarked of his second funeral that it was the only time he'd ever "pall-beared twice for the same man."

But the four stories to which I will devote the main portion of this chapter are of another type than these in regard to what is reportable about the utterance that constitutes the point of the story. They are also among the centerpieces of Mr. Rogers's repertoire in terms of the relish and frequency with which he tells them, and because there are several of them we can begin to distinguish certain formal patterns that will in turn lead us to some larger functional and generic considerations.

I have recorded two tellings of each narrative. For the first story the time intervening between recordings was three years; for the others, ten years. Here are the texts. The titles are my own, supplied for convenience in referring to specific stories (Mr. Rogers does not have formal titles for his stories but generally refers to them as "a story on [name of one of the central characters]").

Drunk Man – I (1979)

Int.:   Oh, the other one I wanted to ask you about was, um . . . what's his name, the man that you bought Bill [a horse] from? Uh . . . I never. . . .

[1]   Motif X111.7 (Thompson 1955–8).

Caswell Rogers: Johnny Fredericks?

Int.:   Yeah! Right, Johnny Fredericks, yeah. . . . I wanted you to tell me about him because he was such a good character.

CR: Well, Johnny was quite a drinker, you know, and uh, he and Cal Markham, uh, went somewhere one day and . . . and told his wife to pick him up at this certain gate to the ranch, and Cal was gonna put him out there and go on home.

So Ms. Brandon was, uh . . . her first husband was Brandon, and he died. And Johnny married her, and he set under her shade trees then.

But anyway, uh, Johnny was awful bad to drink, and Cal put him out.

Why . . . Ms. Brandon was a-waitin' at the gate to pick him up, why, Johnny sort of stumbled around, fell down a time or two, and Ms. Brandon say – right after they was married – Ms. Brandon said, "Why Johnny, you're drunk!"

He said, "Yes, ma'am. You the best judge of a drunk man I ever saw."

Drunk Man – II (1982)

Int.:   Listen, can you . . . will you, um . . . tell me the one about Johnny Fredericks, after he married Ms. Brandon?

CR: Well, Johnny was a little inclined to drink, just a little bit. And, uh . . . he went off to town with Cal Markham one day – they went to Jayton – and Cal lives back this side of Johnny's.

And Johnny told Ms. Brandon to meet him over at their gate, he'd get out there and she'd come over there and get him back at such and such a time of the day, and so Ms. Brandon did.

Johnny got out of the car, why he was so drunk he just fell down.

Ms. Brandon . . . she had . . . he hadn't been married to Ms. Brandon long then. And she said, [sternly] "Why, Johnny, I b'lieve you're drunk!"

Johnny said, "Well, you're a damn good judge of a drunk man."

Not That Young – I (1972)

CR: Jack was a *good* worker and a good cowboy too. He was . . .

Mrs. R.:   And a good drinker.

CR: . . . but he was a little heavy on the bottle. And the old man . . . uh . . . he wanted him to work all the time, and Jack just didn't see any use in that, workin' so much.

One day we were workin' cattle and they had a pole corral . . . a pretty hot day and there's a little bit of shade right around the edge of this pole corral.

Ol' Man Trimble came out and said, "Say," said, "come here,

sit down and rest a little bit," says, "those boys out there are younger'n you are."

I sat down there and Jack was doin' 'bout twice much work as
anybody else out there, and I knew the ol' man and he was . . . been
havin' a pretty hard time, so I told him . . . well, I thought it would
help Jack a little. I said, "Now you see Jack is doin' twice as much
work as anybody out there."

The ol' man said, "Yeah, he sure is, and he's a good hand. I try
to help him and every time I try to help him, why he gets off on one
of these big sprees," and said, "I just can't help a fella like that."

I said, "Well, Mr. Trimble, Jack is *young*," I said. "Probably
you was young one time."

He said, "Hell, yes, but not that young!"

Not That Young – II (1982)

Int.: Well what about um . . . that time you and Mr. Trimble were talking,
um . . . about Jack, you know, and Jack was always goin' out and
gettin' drunk. . . .

CR: Oh, yeah. Jack always, he's gettin' on with some pretty big sprees, and
we was over there workin' cattle and the old man very seldom ever
come on around where we was workin', but he did that day, and they
had a bunch of pole pens, made out of mesquite and cedar poles, and
it was sorta shady.

And the old man said, "Why don't you come over here and sit
down in the shade," said, "those boys are all out there younger'n
you are."

I said, "all right." I sat down there.

But I knew Jack . . . the old man would get mad at Jack 'cause
he'd run off on one o' these sprees, and they'd have troubles. So, I
thought I'd help Jack out and pass a good word to him. Jack was a
good hand in the lot. I never saw a better man in the lot, brandin'
calves. Those days we'd throw 'em all down, work 'em on the ground.

So I told Mr. Trimble, "Now, Mr. Trimble, look at Jack out
there. He's doin' as much work as any two men out there."

"Yup. I know it" [brusquely]. But says, "And I'd like to help
Jack." Said, "Every time I go to help him, he'd go off on one of
these damn sprees," and this, that, and the other, and went on tellin'
me.

And I said, "Yeah, Mr. Trimble, but he's . . . Jack is a young
man now." I said, "Prob'ly one day you was young."

He said, "Hell, yes, but not that young!"

I Should've Left – I (1972)

CR: Well, let's see. . . . We had two old gentlemen lived close to us and
they were both . . . both of 'em were gettin' sorta old.

Mrs. R.: Gentlemen?

CR: They were . . . one of 'em was pretty bad to back in, run into everybody with his car.

 So one day he started to back up and backed into this other ol'
man and bent his car, and he got out and told 'im it was his fault that
the . . . it was his fault and he'd do what he could, he'd straighten
it out for 'im.

 Other old man said, ''No, it was my fault.''

 But he said he didn't see how he could figger that, that he just
backed into 'im.

 He said, ''Well, I knew you's in town – I should've left.''

I Should've Left – II (1982)

CR: Well, these two old gentlemen was both of 'em was gettin' a little old
and they wasn't extry good drivers. But Mr. Trimble'd go to . . .
he's, I guess sorta like I was, just didn't look around much and he'd
just back till he hit somebody, right slow, you know, and then he'd
stop.

 He went to back out and backed into old man Means. Bent his
fender right smart a little bit.

 So he got out and told Mr. Means it was his fault and he wanted
to fix it.

 Mr. Means said, ''No, it wasn't your fault, it was my fault.''

 Mr. Trimble said, ''Well, I don't see how it could be your fault
– I'm the one that run into you.''

 He said, ''Well, I knew you's in town'n' I should've left.''

Pasture Full – I (1972)

Int.: What's that story, that Lawr- . . . that . . . when you and Lawrence
were on the jury and . . . and Shorty Hammond was being tried for
cattle rustling?

CR: Oh, they's tryin' Shorty. Shorty was always into something, and he'd
stole four calves from a fella, so they was tryin' 'im. Lawrence and
I was a prospective jury – they'd already picked the jury, and . . .
but we had to stay there.

 So, uh, 'bout the time they picked the jury, why, Shorty decided,
or his lawyer decided, maybe he better plead guilty; that might be
the easiest way out, because they had the evidence against him.

 So he decided to plead guilty, so the Judge put him on the stand
and got to questioning him and said, ''Mr. Hammond, is it true that
you stole those calves from Mr. Bales?'' (Stole 'em from Ira Bales).

 Said, ''yes.''

 ''Well, Mr. Hammond, don't you know that's wrong to steal cattle?''

 Shorty said, ''yes.''

"Well, why did you do it?"

He said, "Oh, I got drunk, so I didn't know what I's doin'."
Said, "I do that every time I get drunk."

Lawrence said, "Aw, that's no excuse." Said, "I'd have a pasture full if I stole cattle every time I got drunk."

Pasture Full – II (1982)

Int.: Who was it that was on trial for stealin' those cattle when you and Lawrence were on the . . . on the jury?

CR: Oh, that was a fella out here at Red Bluff. He'd, uh, stole some cattle from Ira Bales.

And, uh, so his trial come up, and Lawrence and I both was prospective jurors, but they, uh, didn't pick us. They'd picked . . . got the jury before they got to us.

So, they . . . Shorty Hammond was the boy they was trying. So the Judge asked him how he pleaded and he said, yeah, he'd plead guilty, he stole the cattle.

And he said, "Well, Mr. Hammond, don't you know it's wrong to steal cattle?"

And he said, "Yes, sir, I know it's wrong."

He said, "Well, how come you to steal those cattle?"

He said, "Well I got drunk and I didn't know what I was doin', and stole cattle." Said, "I always steal cattle when I get drunk."

Lawrence sittin' there and said, "Aw, that won't work." Says, "if I stole cattle all the time I . . . every time I got drunk I'd have a pasture full."

Let us attend first to the structure of the stories. In all four, we may observe, the maximally reportable act – that is, the point of the story – is an instance of quoted speech. This bit of quoted speech always occurs at the end and brings the narrative to closure. Erving Goffman has noted that in informal talk, "tales told about experience can (and tend to) be organized from the beginning in terms of what will prove to be the outcome" (1974:559). Taking our lead from this observation, we may profitably examine the organization of the highly end-oriented stories before us in terms of the way in which they set up the climactic reported utterance. As we shall see, however, the punch lines of these stories are reflexive: They loop back to reconstitute, or rekey (Goffman 1974:79–81), what has come before. In this process, the antecedent portion of the narrative, which has built up a context for the punch line, is itself recontextualized. Accordingly, we need to determine both how the punch line is set up and how the portion of the story antecedent to the punch line is made available for such subsequent rekeying.

We may begin by observing that these are stories about morality – proper and improper behavior, responsible and irresponsible action, and attitudes toward them. The moral tenor of the stories is introduced from the beginning;

the first piece of narrative business that is performed in these texts is the introduction of the central actors by reference to the problematic, morally loaded attributes that will make for the focal conflict of the story. While the establishment of character adumbrates the moral tension of the story, the character attributes that are introduced are not bound to the event recounted in the narrative but are antecedent to it, elements of character by which the persons portrayed are more generally known in the community. Whereas the central actors are presented from the beginning in terms of morally colored attributes, the initial section of the stories also serves to bring onto the stage all other interactants in the narrated event who may be implicated in a variety of ways in the central moral conflict.

In addition to the introduction of the dramatis personae, the other function performed by the opening section of the narratives is the setting of the scene for the narrated event to follow. This involves the establishment of the time and place of the central encounter and the occasioning acts or circumstances that bring the dramatis personae into the interaction that will in turn set up the concluding punch line (cf. Chafe 1980a:42; Colby 1973:654; Labov and Waletsky 1967:32).

I draw the introduction of the central actors and the setting of the scene into a single section because they are not always separate and sequentially ordered in the stories. Whereas an element of character is always presented first, not all the dramatis personae are necessarily brought forward before the narrator moves to the setting of the scene. Elements of time, place, or occasioning action may intervene before all the principal actors are finally introduced.

In the first text, the principal character, Johnny Fredericks, is introduced as "quite a drinker." In local terms, this means that unlike others who may drink occasionally, privately, in a controlled way, he is publicly known as one who consistently drinks to excess. The irony of the second version is clear: To identify someone as a drinker in any terms is to indicate that he drinks too much. A person who really drinks "just a little" is not identified in terms of drinking. Likewise, in the first version of "Not That Young" the "little" is ironic; anyone who is at all "heavy on the bottle" is clearly a problem drinker. This irony is not just stylistic, however. There is a strong norm in this culture against direct, bald, on-record negative allegations of any kind, which makes for a tendency to employ irony as a mitigating device (Brown and Levinson 1978:226–7).

In Mr. Rogers's region of West Texas, drinking is the focus of considerable tension and conflict. Public drunkenness especially carries an exaggerated potential for a clash of values and for social disruption: It can lead to violence, bring to the surface religious and ethical divisions in the community, interfere with one's capacity for work (the work ethic is very strong here), and bring embarrassment and shame to the family of the problem drinker.

Thus, when Johnny's wife is introduced, we know in terms of local under-standings that the conflict will center on the public embarrassment the prob-lem drinker brings upon his respectable spouse.

The introduction of Ms.[2] Brandon is bound up with the setting of the scene for the central encounter of the story, which will commence when Johnny is dropped off at the gate to the ranch where, as arranged, his wife is waiting for him. An additional part of the scene-setting function is performed in both versions by the phrase "one day," the first temporal reference in the texts, which situates the narrated event as having occurred at a particular time, in contrast with the character attributes of the dramatis personae, which are not time bound. Also outside the central encounter but bringing the characters into position for it are the various occasioning actions by which the actors converge on the gate to the ranch – Johnny's trip to town and the arrange-ments by which Cal Markham is to drop him off and his wife to pick him up.

The first use of the particle "so" in "and so Ms. Brandon did" (version II) marks the transition from the setting of the scene to the onset of the central action of the story, the narrated event itself. As in much Anglo-American storytelling, "so" operates in Mr. Rogers's stories as a particle that marks sequential process (and sometimes, as here, consequentiality) in the narra-tives. Its use is an indicator that the actions to follow now take place in se-quence and that that sequence is narratively significant.

The first version of the story is somewhat more complicated on the surface, but its structure can be distinguished nevertheless. As in the later version, the first occurrence of "so," in "So Ms. Brandon was, uh . . ." marks what should be the same kind of transition as "so Ms. Brandon did" in version II. What happens, however, is that Mr. Rogers realizes that he is speaking of Johnny *Fredericks's* wife as Ms. *Brandon,* which needs to be accounted for. He does this by noting that "her first husband was Brandon," and that is why he continued to think of her by that name when she remarried later in life.

The reference to Johnny sitting "under her shade trees," although it ap-pears to be nothing more than an amplification of Johnny's sorry character, is actually an interpolation from another of Mr. Rogers's stories involving Johnny. Despite the fact that it did not figure in full in the 1979 recording session, he did tell it in the 1982 session, separated by about fifteen minutes and ten stories from the "Drunk Man" story. Whereas it also centers on quoted speech and implicates the same moral issues as the drunk man story, the shade trees story lacks the punch line that characterizes our other narratives:

> Ol', uh, Dub Geer. Dub was a pretty heavy drinker you know. Dub
> lived up there, same neighborhood. And he'd . . . Dub'd do a lotta
> ridin' and cowboyin' and all, but Dub never did like to do the real
> hard work.

---

[2] Ms. /mɪz/ is used here not as a means of avoiding sexist language, but to reflect local usage.

Dub would tell me every once in a while, he says, "Caswell," said, "we better slow up on this work," says – that was after Ms. Brandon and Johnny married – "Old Man Brandon worked pretty hard, and you see who's sleepin' under those shade trees over there."

In the "Drunk Man" story, the business about the shade trees is a digression, and the return to the main line of the story is marked by the commonly used device, "but anyway," and the recapitulation of Johnny's most salient identity feature – his strong inclination to drink – which would not have been necessary if the digression had not occurred. Mr. Rogers then begins to proceed toward the central encounter, with " 'n' Cal put him out," but he hesitates, I believe, because he has remembered what he was about to say before the digression to explain Ms. Brandon's name – that is, that she was waiting at the gate to pick Johnny up. In other words, "Ms. Brandon was a-waitin' at the gate to pick him up" is a completion of "So Ms. Brandon was . . ." right before the digression, which is where it should have come if it were in its proper structural place, marking the transition between the setting of the scene portion of the narrative and the central encounter.

In the next story, "Not That Young," the dimension of moral conflict is made explicit in the introduction of Jack and "the old man," who is his grandfather. Jack, like Johnny, is a drinker – publicly known as one, as witness Mrs. Rogers's interjection – and although he is capable of good work his moral worth is compromised by the fact that he often chooses to go off on binges instead. Thus, because the old man wants him to work all the time and Jack goes off on sprees, his drinking, like Johnny's, brings about conflict within the family, a serious problem. In the second of the two versions, only Jack's character is described in explicit terms, but it is clear to the auditors that they are working at his grandfather's place ("over there"), which means working his grandfather's cattle. That is, the old man is a cattleman, a cattle owner, which implies a certain economic substance and status, whereas Jack, who simply works for him, goes off on sprees. The moral contrast between the two is strongly implicit. Mr. Rogers himself is the third character in the story, and one of the two central interactants.

The scene of the story is set once again by references to time ("One day" and "that day"), place (Mr. Trimble's cow lot, made up of pole pens), and occasioning action. The latter, which functions to bring together the principal actors in the narrative, is the "working" of Mr. Trimble's cattle: the branding, ear marking, dehorning, inoculation, and castration of his new calves. After this introduction, the story proceeds to a recounting of the central narrative event.

In the "Pasture Full" story, Shorty is identified at the beginning as a cattle thief, the moral valence of which needs no comment in this cattle ranching community. In the earlier version of the story, his character as a trouble maker is amplified by identifying him as someone who is "always into something," a euphemism for always doing things that cause trouble. He is, in short, identified as a disruptive person. Lawrence is set up as the morally contrasting figure. That he is a prospective member of the jury for Shorty's trial implies that he is a respectable, upstanding member of the community.

The scene is set in the courtroom, and the presence of the interactants is accounted for, with Shorty as defendant and Lawrence and Mr. Rogers as prospective jurors required to remain after the jury has been selected. As before, the particle "so" marks a sequential movement toward the central narrated event. In the first version, "So, uh, 'bout the time . . ." begins to situate the narrative event temporally and leads into the further occasioning act represented by "so he decided to plead guilty." The next "so" ("so the Judge put him on the stand") marks the transition from the setting of the scene to the onset of the narrated event itself. In version II, we have another series of three "so's": first "so his trial came up"; then "So they . . . ," which turns out to be a false start as Mr. Rogers realizes that we need Shorty's name because it features in the subsequent dialog; and finally "So the Judge asked him how he pleaded," which marks the transition from the setting of the scene to the narrated event.

In the remaining story, "I Should've Left," the central actors are presented to us as two old men who are negligent, dangerous drivers. In the first version, we are told explicitly about only one of them, but the suggestion is present that the other one may have a similar problem inasmuch as he is equally old. Then too, the false start, "They were . . . one of 'em was . . ." may indicate that the narrator thinks of them both in the same terms. This impression would be sustained later, when both claim responsibility for the mishap. In the later version, the opening makes explicit that both men are bad drivers, though by use of ironic understatement: "They wasn't extry good drivers."

The scene-setting function is very minimally attended to in this story. Indeed, it is lacking entirely in the second version. In the earlier version, this function is served only by the time-situating phrase "So one day," which also marks the transition to the central narrated event.

Let us summarize. We have seen that the initial section of each of these four anecdotes is devoted to the fulfillment of two complementary functions, the introduction of the dramatis personae and the setting of the scene for the narrated event to follow. To this point in our examination of the narratives, several things have been accomplished:

1. The central actors have been introduced in terms of morally weighted attributes that they bring with them to the narrated event, and most of the secondary characters have been introduced as well.

A variable combination of the following scene-setting functions has been presented:

2. The narrated event has been situated in place.
3. The dramatis personae have been brought onto the scene of the narrated event by certain occasioning actions or circumstances.
4. The story has been situated in time by the use of time markers, such as "one day."
5. In several of the stories, a process of narrative sequentiality has been set in motion toward the onset of the narrated event, marked by the sequential (and sometimes consequential) particle "so."

We are ready, now, to turn to a consideration of the narrated event itself, the sequence of actions and reactions that is actually replayed for us in the narrative and toward which the introductory section has led. We have already noted that the essential part of the narrated event is the conversational encounter that culminates in the punch line, but this portion of the narrative may include other elements as well. Thematically, the narrated event always implicates a moral offense, which then provides the focus for the conversational encounter that concludes the narrative. In formal terms, the narrated event is made up of reported action that

1. Always includes quoted speech as part of the conversational encounter.
2. May include indirect discourse or other forms of reported speech.
3. May also include other nonverbal action.

In all cases, the narrated event concludes with a dialogic exchange culminating in the quoted speech of the punch line.

The moral offense around which the narrated event revolves has already been adumbrated in the opening section of the story in which the principal actors are presented in terms of particular morally weighted attributes. In two of the stories, the offense takes place within the narrated event itself and is presented to us as part of reported action. In the "Drunk Man" story, it is Johnny's visibly drunken, out-of-control behavior: He is so drunk that he stumbles around and falls down in the presence of his respectable wife and his neighbor. This is a physical, not a verbal, act. The same is true of the offense in "I Should've Left," which consists of Mr. Trimble's backing into and damaging Mr. Means's car; he is a bad and negligent driver and should not be driving at all, endangering the property and safety of others. In the two remaining stories, the morally offensive actions have taken place antecedent to the narrated event, namely, Shorty's stealing of the cattle in "Pasture Full" and Jack's going off on sprees when he should have been working in "Not That Young."

In "Pasture Full," the narrated event is composed wholly of the reported or quoted speech of the trial proceedings. Part of the account is very summary; "the Judge put him on the stand" may not be readily apparent as reported speech, but it is in fact a summary of the verbal routine by which the defendant is called to the stand. The next action, "got to questioning him," is also summary, but here the speech act involved is explicitly named. From this point on, the story consists entirely of quoted speech with its associated framing devices.

"Not That Young" is somewhat more complicated. After the opening act of quoted speech, in which Mr. Trimble calls Mr. Rogers over to sit down and Rogers responds to the summons, the story shifts away from the conversational interaction momentarily as Mr. Rogers tells us more about the background of the exchange to follow. The essential point here is that Mr. Rogers is a spokesman for Jack's position in the conflict between Jack and his grandfather; Jack is not a direct interactant in the reported encounter, but his present behavior within the frame of the narrated event does influence the conversational interaction between Mr. Trimble and Mr. Rogers. Accordingly, in version I we are given an account of Jack's relevant action within the narrated event. In version II, we receive information on Jack's qualities as a worker, given to us in the introductory section of the earlier version as part of the introduction of the dramatis personae. In both cases, this additional information is to account for Mr. Rogers's motivation for taking the tack he does in the ensuing dialogue with Mr. Trimble. The information is reserved for this point in the narrative because it does not become relevant until Mr. Trimble calls him over. Only then does his idea of smoothing things out between the old man and his grandson come into play. The sequential particle "so" in "So, I thought it would help Jack" (version II) shows that his motivation is actually a part of the temporal sequence of the narrative.

We arrive, then, at the conversational encounter itself, the core of these anecdotes. As we move into the conversational encounter, an important shift takes place in the presentational mode of the stories, a shift from the recounting of circumstances and actions – telling about them – to replaying the actions, reenacting them to a degree by ostensibly – and ostensively – repeating what was done in the original past event of which the narrative is an account (cf. McDowell 1982). In the terminology of classic rhetoric, this may be seen as a shift along the continuum from diegesis to mimesis, from telling to showing. By far most of the reported turns at talk in the stories are rendered as direct discourse, in which the reported speech is actually quoted. To be sure, the mimetic closeness with which the original dialogue is replayed is attenuated by the quotative devices that frame the direct discourse, but the retention of the tense of the original quoted utterance – a basic feature of direct discourse – enhances the sense of reenactment by transposing the past into the present. And at times, in two of the stories, the framing devices fall away and the quoted speech is left to stand on its own.[3]

---

[3] I am using the term "mimetic" here solely to identify a presentational mode, with no claims implied concerning the degree of actual correspondence between the original event and its representation in narrative discourse. In the process, I am begging some very large issues (for an excellent discussion, see Sternberg 1982).

Direct discourse predominates in these anecdotes as the means by which the turns at talk that make up the narrated event are reported. The "Drunk Man" story has two turns at talk in each version, all of which are in direct discourse; "Not That Young" has five turns per version, all once again in direct discourse, although one turn shifts in mid-course to indirect; "Pasture Full" has seven turns per version, with all seven in the first version being direct discourse while the second version begins with two turns in indirect discourse before shifting to direct; and "I Should've Left" has four turns per version, evenly divided between direct and indirect in the first version and weighted three to one in favor of direct discourse in the later one. It is worth noting that the use of indirect discourse tends to occur in the opening turns at talk, soon followed by a shift to direct discourse for the remainder of the dialogue. The indirect discourse, I would suggest, represents an intermediate step in the movement from telling about to reenacting. Thus in the second version of "Pasture Full," for example, the first turn is indirect ("So the Judge asked him how he pleaded"), the second is free indirect (transitional from indirect to direct) ("he said, yeah, he'd plead guilty, he stole the cattle"), and the concluding five turns are direct. In version II of "I Should've Left," we see a similar pattern, in which the first turn at talk is given in indirect discourse ("So he got out and told Mr. Means it was his fault . . .") and the concluding three in direct discourse.

As suggested earlier, even direct discourse is kept at a remove from full reenactment of the purported dialogue of the original event by the quotative devices with which it is framed. Reported speech, especially quoted speech, involves special problems of communicative management, because the narrator is actually speaking for other people in addition to himself. Accordingly, there is a need for ways of marking the difference between the voice of the narrator in the present storytelling context and the reported speech of the actors in the original event being reported (one of whom can be the person who later tells the story, but in a different voice), and of marking speaker change within the conversational dialogue that is the core of the narrated event. The quotative frames are an important means of accomplishing these tasks.

An essential constituent of the quotative frames is the *verbum dicendi*, the verb of saying. In the stories before us, the *verba dicendi* used to introduce the quoted speech of direct discourse are overwhelmingly forms of "to say," either in the past tense ("said") or the historical present ("says"), of which there are only two instances. These forms aside, the only other verb of saying used with direct discourse is "told," used once in the second version of "Not That Young" to frame a slightly more emphatic utterance than "said" would convey (and once as a false start in the same text). For indirect discourse, the *verba dicendi* are similarly limited: two instances of "told," one of "tellin' " (historical present), one of "asked," and two of "said." These are all conspicuously neutral toward the reported speech they frame, consistent, as we shall see, with the ultimate moral impact of the stories.

It is noteworthy that forms of "to say" may be used both turn-initially, to mark the opening of direct discourse or a change in speaker, and turn-internally, to segment a single utterance. In the latter case, the quoted utterance is always made up of more than one sentence, with both sentences generally, but not necessarily, set off by the quotative verbs but connected by cohesive ties (more on this later). We may also observe that the quotative verbs may be used with or without a subject. The omission of the subject before "said," or "says," is not uncommon in American vernacular storytelling; other devices, as follows, serve to disambiguate the dialogue.

In addition to the *verba dicendi*, there is a further range of devices which serve to organize the reported speech of these stories. In fact, the organizing system for reported speech in these texts is highly redundant, with multiple devices operating concurrently to indicate who is speaking and when. Most of these can be illustrated from the dialogue in the earlier version of "Pasture Full":

> so the Judge put him on the stand and got to questioning him and said, "Mr. Hammond, is it true that you stole those calves from Mr. Bales?" (Stole 'em from Ira Bales).
> Said, "yes."
> "Well, Mr. Hammond, don't you know that's wrong to steal cattle?"
> Shorty said, "yes."
> "Well, why did you do it?"
> He said, "Oh, I got drunk, so I didn't know what I's doin'."
> Said, "I do that every time I get drunk."
> Lawrence said, "Aw, that's no excuse." Said, "I'd have a pasture full if I stole cattle every time I got drunk."

First of all, reported speech may be attributed. The speaker may be identified by a variety of means: by pronoun ("he said"), by name ("Shorty said"), or by some other identifying term ("the Judge . . . said"). Similarly, reported speech may be addressed to an identified addressee, as in "Well, Mr. Hammond. . . ." Third, the beginnings of quoted utterances may be marked by particles such as "Well," "Oh," or "Aw," that tend to occur only in this initial position, whereas the ends of these utterances are marked by transitional pauses that are longer than those that may occur within quoted utterances. And fourth, the conversational encounter may be organized by recognizable conversational structures and routines, such as the routine of courtroom interrogation in the passage above, made up of question and answer adjacency pairs. This routine serves so well in assisting us to differentiate among speakers that two of the quoted turns at talk are replayed without recourse to any quotative frames at all.

Two further organizational devices, not present in the above passage from "Pasture Full," may be illustrated from the "Drunk Man" story. Mr. Rogers does not resort very often to the taking on of special voices for expressive purposes, but he does so in both versions of this anecdote in presenting the speech of Ms. Brandon in her indignant challenge of her drunken husband. Thus her "Why, Johnny, you're drunk!" is rendered in a markedly higher pitch, more loudly, and in a more clipped manner than Johnny's speech or the rest of the surrounding discourse, clearly differentiating Ms. Brandon's voice from Johnny's. The only other quoted utterances in our corpus that are paralinguistically set off in this manner are the punch lines of both versions of "Not That Young." Finally, we may find in the concluding line of the first version of the "Drunk Man" story the use of an anaphoric tie that marks Johnny's utterance as a response to what precedes it, made by a different speaker; his first word, "yes," marks assent to or agreement with Ms. Brandon's challenge.

Whereas cohesive ties such as this may be found throughout the replayed dialogues in these stories, helping give coherence to the interactions portrayed, in three of the four stories, including "Drunk Man," cohesion assumes special stylistic importance when we get to the punch line that brings the narratives to closure. With the exception of "I Should've Left," the last lines of the stories are saturated with anaphoric ties to the lines that precede them to a far greater degree than at any other point in the stories. A demonstration of these ties (based on Halliday and Hasan 1976) will open the way to a more extensive discussion of the role of the punch line in these anecdotes, toward which much of our analysis has been directed.

Let us continue to examine the "Drunk Man" story. Here again are the last two lines of the dialogue between Johnny and his wife:

> Ms. Brandon said, "Why Johnny, you're drunk!"
> He said, "Yes ma'am. You the best judge of a drunk man I ever saw."

We can identify at least six ties between these two brief lines:

1. The quotative frames, "Ms. Brandon said" and "He said," are in parallel construction.
2. Johnny's "Yes ma'am," as noted above, marks assent to the preceding utterance, or at least acknowledgment of it.
3. Both quoted utterances open with terms of address.
4. Ms. Brandon's challenge and Johnny's response are in parallel construction: You're X/You('re) Y.
5. Johnny's "best judge" names and evaluates the illocutionary force of Ms. Brandon's challenge.
6. The use of the key word "drunk" in both utterances is an instance of lexical repetition.

The second version lacks the tie of assent and the parallelism of the opening term of address but carries over the other cohesive ties that we find in the earlier one.

In "Not That Young," the patterns of cohesion show up more strongly when we note that the penultimate line is itself made up of two segments, marked by the repetition of the quotative frame, "I said." If we break the line down into the two resultant shorter segments, we find that the punch line has strong anaphoric ties to both of them, intensifying the sense of cohesion across the concluding lines of the dialogue.

> I said, "Well, Mr. Trimble, Jack is young,"
> I said, "probably you was young one time."
> He said, "Hell, yes, but not that young!"

An inventory of the cohesive ties between the punch line and what precedes it would include the following:

1. The parallelism of the opening quotative frame: I said (2×)/He said
2. The rhyme of the particle that opens the quoted utterances: Hell:Well
3. The assent marked by "yes," probably to both parts of Mr. Rogers's statement, but certainly to the suggestion that he "was young one time"
4. The contradiction marked by the adversative conjunction "but," qualifying the assent of the "yes" that precedes it
5. The contrastive demonstrative "not that," qualifying the assent concerning his earlier youth still further
6. The lexical repetition of the key word "young"

The second version of "Not That Young" employs the same range of cohesive ties as this one, with the exception of the rhyming opening particles.

Like the penultimate line in "Not That Young," the quoted utterances in both concluding turns at talk in "Pasture Full" are divided into two segments, each introduced by the quotative frame. Here, though, despite the fact that both lines are relatively long, the patterns of cohesion extend across the whole lines.

> He said, "Oh, I got drunk, so I didn't know what I's doin'." Said, "I do that every time I get drunk."
>
> Lawrence said, "Aw, that's no excuse." Said, "I'd have a pasture full if I stole cattle every time I got drunk."

The ties include the following:

1. The parallelism of the initial quotative frame
2. The parallelism of the particles "Oh" and "Aw" that open the quoted utterances

3. The demonstrative reference ''that's,'' which points back to the preceding line
4. The adjective ''no,'' which repudiates an aspect of the preceding line
5. The naming of the illocutionary force of Shorty's preceding statement, namely, ''excuse''
6. The repetition of the medial quotative frame, ''Said''
7. The substitution of ''stole cattle'' for ''that'' in Shorty's statement
8. The parallelism of the entire concluding phrase, varying only the tense of ''get''
9. The lexical repetition of ''drunk,'' which is tied to both uses of the word in the penultimate line

Here again, the second version displays a similar pattern, which by now will be apparent to the reader.

The fourth story, by contrast with those we have just examined, lacks the density of cohesion that links the concluding lines of the dialogue in the others. Nevertheless, in the second version, we may observe once again the parallelism of the initial quotative frame and the I–you–I pronoun alternation in both lines.

Let us examine the effect of the strong cohesion between the punch lines of the stories and the preceding lines that set them up. It would not be too strong to say that density and multiplicity of the ties between them sets the concluding lines of the stories off to a degree from the rest of the text and gives them the quality of a kind of closing couplet. The multiple repetitions, parallel constructions, and other forms of anaphora contribute directly to the strong sense of closure that is achieved by the punch lines (Smith 1968:158–71). When the punch line is spoken, we know that the story is complete simply in formal terms.

The cohesion between the punch line and the line that comes before it is such that the punch line impresses us as a transformation of the preceding line – similar to it and modeled upon it, but transforming it in the process. The punch line contains within it two voices – its own and that of the preceding speaker upon which it has wrought a transformation. Most important, this double-voicedness is a correlative on the formal level of the double-voicedness of the punch line on the level of meaning as well. That is, the formal nature of the punch line is a correlative of its fundamentally ironic function. To demonstrate this, we need to examine the content and social interactional structure of the reported conversational encounters that lead to and culminate in the punch lines of the stories.

We may begin by recalling that these anecdotes are moral stories; the conversations are about moral issues: decorum, responsibility, work, order. How are these issues developed in the interactions between the principal actors?

In "Drunk Man," the exchange between Johnny and Ms. Brandon is occasioned by the strained situation in which Ms. Brandon is confronted in the view of a neighbor by her visibly drunk husband. In interactional terms, her accusation, "Why Johnny, you're drunk!" is a challenge in Labov and Fanshel's sense, "a reference . . . to a situation, which if true, would lower the status of the other person" (1977:64). Her challenge, while face-threatening (cf. Brown and Levinson 1978) to Johnny, is a small attempt at face-saving for her, by displaying her moral condemnation of his drunken state.

It is within this context, then, that Johnny's own response may be seen as artful and reportable. What makes it so noteworthy is the telling effectiveness with which it rekeys the situation, in Goffman's sense (1974). Ms. Brandon's challenge places Johnny and his behavior directly in the spotlight of moral evaluation, with a threat to his social face. What can he do? He can't deny that he is drunk; indeed, he acknowledges it in passing with his "Yes, Ma'am." But then he goes on deftly to deflect the challenge by turning the spotlight elsewhere. In one sentence, he transforms the situation into one in which it is not he but his wife who is being evaluated – the judged, ironically, becomes the judger. What is at issue now is not his condition, but her competence as a judge of it. Moreover, his judgment is sarcastically favorable, a kind of mocking ratification of her ability to judge the obvious. If she denies it, she has undermined her authority to challenge him in the first place. If she accepts it – and in terms of the story her acceptance is at least implicit, because we hear no more from her – she has collaborated at least tacitly in Johnny's evasive rekeying of the situation. Johnny's response involves still another evasive stratagem: His wife is being evaluated not as a judge of him in particular but of an impersonal abstract drunk man. Johnny disappears into the class. He is portrayed then as verbally snatching a kind of victory from the jaws of defeat by rescuing his face in a situation in which it appeared that he has lost it. Yet for all that, his response is so effectively "right," it does not undermine – indeed, it ratifies – that Ms. Brandon is right too in challenging him for his moral offense.

Turning to "Not That Young," we find that it is artfully constructed from the very beginning in terms of a set of paired contrasts between youth and age and working and avoiding work. In the narrated event, these contrasts are evoked by the old man, Mr. Trimble, when he calls Mr. Rogers over to rest in the shade while Jack, who is "younger'n you are" and doing "twice as much work as any man out there" continues to work. Whereas Mr. Rogers, knowing of the friction between grandfather and grandson, takes the opportunity to speak on Jack's behalf, Mr. Trimble, from his place in the shade, criticizes Jack, who is working especially effectively, for occasionally going off on sprees; this is one of the major ironies of the story. Rogers, in turn, attempts to account for Jack's irresponsibility by attributing it to his youth, the same youth that enables him to work so vigorously. Young men will be irresponsible at times, but at least this is compensated for in Jack's case by his ability to do the work of two men when he does work. Then, using the rhetorical strategy of identification, Rogers points out that Mr. Trimble was young once too, and here Mr. Trimble is caught, for he was known in the community for his own escapades and was fully as "young" as Jack. What is more, people knew it.

From this vantage point, the latter half of Mr. Trimble's response, "but not that young," appears on the surface as an after-the-fact gesture at upholding the position he has been taking as a spokesman for sobriety and responsibility, but it is understood by Mr. Rogers as an acknowledgment by the old man of the inconsistency of his attitude toward Jack. In explaining the story to me, Mr. Rogers made clear that he sees Mr. Trimble in the punch line as in effect stepping back from the line he has sustained throughout the exchange and rereading the situation and his own stance toward it. The punch line amounts to a concession that he knows he is taking the situation too seriously; it objectifies the situation and assumes a relativist stance. Not that work and responsibility aren't valid ideals – they are – but one has to recognize that life doesn't – perhaps shouldn't – always work that way.

"Pasture Full" works to similar effect. In this story, the interaction of the narrated event is organized in terms of the routine of interrogating a defendant in a court of law. Clear contrasts are operating in the story between the agents of morality and the legal order, namely, the Judge and jury, and the morally culpable defendant, a confessed thief.

The interaction proceeds with the Judge doing the questioning and Shorty, having decided to plead guilty, doing the remedial work of acknowledging the wrongness of his act. Ironically, though, what Shorty offers as a mitigating factor in his guilt actually casts him in a light that is worse yet: Not only is he a thief, but a drunkard as well. We have already established the strong tension surrounding drunkenness in this region.

Right after Shorty's confession of his double moral lapse comes the response by Lawrence that serves as the punch line. Lawrence, as a prospective juryman, aligned with the agents of morality and order against the hapless defendant, says "Aw, that's no excuse. I'd have a pasture full if I stole cattle every time I got drunk," suggesting, albeit with some joking exaggeration, that he often gets drunk himself. At one level, this statement plays on the ambivalence felt in this region toward alcohol; Lawrence likes to drink, sometimes even to excess, but he doesn't let himself get out of control the way Shorty does. Most important, however, his statement shifts the moral alignment in the courtroom: Lawrence is now identified with Shorty, as someone who gets drunk, even while denying the validity of Shorty's excuse, which is, of course, truly "no excuse." By his words, he has broken the moral alignment that has prevailed and rearranged it, reframed the situation. Again, he does not deny that Shorty is guilty and behaved wrongly – he just sets up a relativistic alternative concerning what can be morally acceptable in real life, regardless of ideal public standards.

The remaining story, "I Should've Left," differs from the others insofar as its punch line lacks the intensity of cohesion with the line that precedes it that characterizes the stories we have already considered. Notwithstanding this lack of formal correspondence, however, this last story is very much like the others in the effect of its punch line to rekey the situation that has seemed to prevail, to accomplish an ironic shift in our understanding of what it is that is going on in the narrated event and the attitudes of the principal actors toward it.

The narrated event opens with the crisis of the car wreck, as Mr. Trimble, no longer able to drive responsibly, backs into Mr. Means. The first interactional move that takes place, though, following on Mr. Trimble's offense, is his appropriately redressive admission of culpability and offer of compensation for the damage. When Mr. Means follows with what seems like his own claim of responsibility for the accident, the exchange begins to take on the air of a politeness display. This seems all the more apparent as Mr. Trimble in turn insists that it was *his* fault: He was the one who backed into Mr. Means. And it is at this point, as our impression seems to be confirmed, that Mr. Means overturns things with his punch line: "Well, I knew you's in town – I should've left." He is not being polite to Mr. Trimble at all but is rather underscoring his culpability. Trimble is notorious as a bad driver, but one who persists in driving anyway; anyone with good sense would stay out of his vicinity, and anyone who does not give him a wide berth deserves the blame for whatever disasters might ensue. The meaning of Mr. Means's challenge is all the more telling because it is expressed through indirection. He has remained polite on the surface, but his politeness is ironic, a means of conveying strong criticism (Brown and Levinson 1978:234, 267–70) in a way far more memorable and reportable than a direct imputation of Mr. Trimble's culpability would have been.

Now that our analytical path through these anecdotes has led us to an understanding in formal and functional terms of the efficacy of the punch lines that bring them to closure, we can see more clearly just how tightly structured these stories are. The punch line is the critical element, the point of the story. But the punch line in turn depends closely on the line that precedes it and on the social interactional and substantive thrust of the entire replayed conversation that constitutes the core of the narrated event. All these elements are rooted in a particular moral tension that is the subject of the conversational interaction, giving the punch line its ironic and relativistic impact; this tension is adumbrated from the very beginning of the story in the introduction of the dramatis personae. Thus, from the introduction of the principal actors, to the setting of the scene that brings them to the central encounter, to the conver-

sational interaction between them, to the punch line that caps it off, the parts
of these anecdotes constitute a markedly tight structure.

These tight formal and functional constraints, centering around quoted
speech, may account for the notable stability and consistency of these stories
over time. The paired versions of the four stories in our corpus were told over
an interval of three years in one case and ten full years in the others, yet they
remain remarkably close to each other in form. In each case we find the same
overall structure, closely similar introductory matter, the same narrated event,
and closely similar reported conversations, including the same number of turns
at talk and two concluding lines that vary only slightly, if at all, across the
two versions.

The stability of these stories over time may be highlighted by contrasting
them with other closely related narratives told by Mr. Rogers. Here are two
renditions of another narrative about Mr. Trimble and his grandson Jack dealing with their ongoing conflict; as before, Mr. Trimble wants Jack to work
like a responsible and reliable person and Jack would far rather go off on
sprees. These texts were recorded in the same conversations as the others, the
first in 1972 and the second ten years later.

Three Day Spree – I (1972)
Int.:   What were the. . . . There was another thing about Jack. What was it?
        He went one time for three days or somethin'!
CR: Oh yeah. //They's cuttin' wheat.
Mrs. R.:   //One time?
CR: They's cuttin' wheat and the combine broke down and couldn't get a
        part – you had to have it welded.
        So he went to town to get it welded and he got off on one o' these
        sprees and was gone three days and the old man was just throwin' a
        fit. That wheat was in the field, ripe, ready to cut, you know, Jack
        would be home in about three days.

Three-Day Spree – II (1982)
CR: One day I met Mr. Trimble in the road over here, and he said, "Say,"
        he says, uh "have you seen Jack?"
        I said, "no, I haven't . . . I don't believe I've seen him for two
        or three days."
        And he said, "By God, I haven't either." Says, "we was cuttin'
        wheat out here and broke the binder down and, uh, he went to get a
        piece welded – he couldn't buy a new one and went to get a piece
        welded – and he's been gone three days with the damn thing in his
        car," and it was fixin' to rain and he's in terrible shape.

In these stories, unlike the others we have been considering, it is clearly
the circumstance that is most reportable, not what was said. The 1982 version

employs quoted speech as a stylistic device to organize a substantial part of the story, but it is not at all necessary, as witness the earlier text, in which the episode is recounted with no quoted speech whatsoever. In the narratives in which the point of the story is an instance of quoted speech, something someone said, the narrated event remains constant over time, namely, the conversational encounter that culminates in the punch line. This is not the case in these two stories. In the earlier version, the narrated event is a third-person account about Jack going off with the combine part and his grandfather's distress at his prolonged absence. In the 1982 telling, the narrated event is a first-person encounter between Mr. Rogers and Mr. Trimble. There is, thus, considerable variance in the form of these latter narratives across tellings. I would suggest, then, that when quoted speech is the focus of the narrative and a particular utterance is the very point of it, the text is formally more constrained and less susceptible to change from one telling to the next.

Let us return to our consideration of our original four anecdotes. In each case, we have seen, the anecdotes achieve their effect by rekeying the situation, overturning the apparent direction of the interaction and the moral alignments and attitudes that have seemed to control it and establishing an ironic alternative, not as a substitute but as a coexistent perspective. The effect of the punch line is to that extent subversive, a breakthrough both on the part of the one who is reported to have spoken it and on the part of the narrator into a kind of skepticism and relativism that takes pleasure in refusing to take ideal, normative moral expectations too seriously – a "comic corrective," in Burke's apt phrase, "containing two-way attributes lacking in polemical, one-way approaches to social necessity" (1937:213).

This, in fact, is the essence of much humor. Indeed, upon examination, these stories may be seen to have some basic affinities with other humorous expressive forms. The punch line in many narrative jokes built upon reported speech, for example, works by reframing what has come before it (Sherzer 1985), and traditional circus clown routines (Bouissac 1976:167) operate in a manner quite similar to Johnny's encounter with his wife, "the juxtaposition of a control against that which is controlled, this juxtaposition being such that the latter triumphs" (Douglas 1968:365). In all, the "successful subversion of one form by another completes or ends the joke, for it changes the balance of power" (ibid.). To carry the correspondences still further, traditional verbal jokes also represent a form of reported speech. They are often introduced by reference to the person from whom they were learned, as in "Wanna hear a joke my sister told me?" (cf. Sacks 1974), and insofar as they are known to be in oral tradition they are in a sense reported out of the abstract collective voice of tradition. And again, as noted, many narrative jokes employ fictional reported speech both as stylistic device and as punch line.

Given all these correspondences between jokes and other humorous routines and the anecdotes of our West Texas storyteller, what are the differences

among them? Part of the answer to this question is suggested by a consideration of the context in which these stories occur. They are conventionally told
in a variety of small-group sociable settings, such as intervals between collective work tasks, gatherings at the barber shop or cotton gin or drugstore, and
so on, in which the conversation deals with the members of the local community and the surrounding region. In recent years, they have figured most
prominently during visits by the narrator to members of his family who have
moved away from home or on occasions when those relatives have come back
on visits of their own. Conversation on such occasions often involves catching
up on the people of the community – births, deaths, marriages, divorces (in
recent years) and other significant activities. The community is small, and the
ranching and farming region around it is rather thinly populated. People are
still identified in terms of residence ("Cal lived back this side of Johnny's")
and kin connections ("Ms. Brown, you know was one of 'em – Joe Bob's
mother"), with the latter providing one of the major organizing principles by
which successive people are brought up for mention and discussion. Of course,
kinship is not the only salient social feature by which people are known; as in
most small, traditional, agrarian communities the personal and social identity
of individuals is also defined in part by their actions and experiences, elements of their local social biography.

It is here that narrative comes into play; stories are the major means by
which such actions and experiences are memorialized and given expression.
Thus, the mention of a given individual may evoke a story about him or her,
either a personal narrative in which the teller figures with that individual, or
a third-person narrative about the individual in question that has been told to
the narrator by someone else at varying degrees of remove from the original
event. That is, the chain of transmission may be of varying length, but there
is always a sense of locality and familiarity about the dramatis personae of
the stories – they are all known personally or in terms of their connections
within the community: kinfolk, neighbors, friends.

Because these stories are about known and familiar people and constitute
a part of their social biographies, they are densely indexical in a concrete social
sense. That is, part of their meaning derives from the great complex of indexical associations that they evoke – the people portrayed, other known aspects
of their lives and characters, and potentially everyone in the community, including those present at the storytelling event, with whom they are linked by
the kinds of social and communicative ties that give cohesion to the conversations in which the stories are told.

To be sure, these stories, like all literature used as equipment for living
(Burke 1941), have a certain metaphorical as well as metonymic meaning
(Stewart 1982:34–5), as a kind of extended name or label for the recurrent
social problem situations they portray: the embarrassment occasioned by publicly visible immoral behavior, the damaging of someone else's property through

careless incompetence, and so on. And to extend the Burkean perspective still further, the stories also convey an attitude toward such situations and a strategy for dealing with them. The attitudes will vary depending on the situation, but there is always an attendant uneasiness about the public moral conflict the stories portray; the favored strategy that emerges from the stories is to alleviate the resultant tension by ironically transforming the ongoing situation into something else.

It is here that we see the importance of the crucial bits of quoted speech that bring the stories to closure; what is highlighted in these anecdotes is the transformative capacity of speech. Bakhtin maintains that "The speaking person in the novel is always to one degree or another, an *ideologue,* and his words are always *ideologemes.* . . . It is precisely as ideologemes that discourse becomes the object of representation in the novel" (1981:333, emphasis in the original). So too in these anecdotes, but the ideology to which the last speaker gives voice is ultimately ironic and skeptical (White 1973:37), although never overtly critical or condemnatory, showing how the normative pressures of morality that lead to social tension may be evaded by those with the verbal wit to do so.

Traditional punch line jokes, as many have pointed out, have the same subversive potential. Unlike our anecdotes, however, jokes are not at all rooted in community; they are anonymous, impersonal, and generalized. Indeed, if one were inclined toward speculation, one might suggest that the modern punch line joke, which emerged as a recognized form only in the nineteenth century (Röhrich 1977:4, 8), might have evolved out of the punch line anecdote under the social conditions of the modern industrial era. Anecdotes of the kind we have been examining thrive in the intimate social environment of the small local community, whereas jokes belong preeminently to the impersonal milieu of urban industrial society (Röhrich 1977:9). As imaginative products ungrounded in a known community of real individuals, jokes can only be metaphorical and speculative in their relationship to actual experience. They tell us in hypothetical terms about how structures *might* fall apart or be overturned, whereas the true anecdotes are told to keep us aware of the vulnerability of life as it really *is* and the capacity of speech both to make this vulnerability apparent and to bring it under control.[4]

---

[4] A shorter, preliminary version of this chapter appeared in Bauman (1984).

5

"I GO INTO MORE DETAIL NOW, TO BE SURE"

Narrative variation and the shifting contexts of traditional storytelling

Introduction

Perhaps the most basic and persistent problem confronted by students of oral literature is gauging the effect of the interplay of tradition and innovation, persistence and change, as manifested in the oral text. I have already touched on this problem in my analysis of reported speech in a series of West Texas oral anecdotes (Chapter 4), which revealed that those narratives in which quoted speech served as a kind of punch line were markedly more stable over time than those in which an instance of quoted speech was not the point of the story. For much of the history of modern folklore scholarship, the scales in which folklorists have weighed this dynamic interplay between tradition and innovation have been overbalanced rather strongly in favor of traditionality and persistence. Tradition has been the privileged term, consistent with the larger frames of reference predominant in social thought that have held the folk – peasants and primitives – to be conservative, "tradition bound," resistant to change, and so on (Bauman 1977c, 1982; Ben-Amos 1972).

The past couple of decades, however, have witnessed an accelerating shift in perspectives on the dynamics of folklore that have begun to redress the imbalance. The recent burgeoning of a performance-centered perspective, especially, has brought with it a growing awareness of the role of individual creativity in oral literature and of texts as situated and emergent within particular contexts (Bauman 1977b; Ben-Amos and Goldstein 1975; Paredes and Bauman 1972).

One line of inquiry fostered by these new concerns has been the study of the individual performer, now beginning to replace the anonymous collectivity as the focus of folkloristic attention in explorations of the social base of folklore. Albert Lord's seminal study, *The Singer of Tales* (1960), for example, opens a range of productive questions in this regard: the constitution of the individual repertoire, the acquisition of performance skills, the individual's performance career, differences across performances of what a singer considers "the same song," and so on. But progress in pursuing these various lines of inquiry has been uneven. Lord's own study, for all the criticisms and misuses to which it has been subjected, establishes a model for the close formal analysis of oral texts as a basis for the comparison of texts across multiple performances of a specific singer. As yet, though, we do not have similarly closely focused comparisons across successive tellings of spoken narratives, which are less rigorously marked by formal poetic conventions of meter and line construction than Lord's epics, however highly patterned they may be.

I should emphasize that I am speaking of the close comparison of spoken narratives in terms of the formal structures of the narrative discourse and in relation to context. Those few studies that have tracked individual folktale narrators through successive tellings of their tales have concentrated on rather impressionistic analysis of changes in plot, motifs, and other aspects of content, with relatively little attention to discourse form or context (see, e.g., Brunvand 1961; Crowley 1966:108–13; discussion in Dégh 1969:177–9). Recent developments in the formal analysis of narrative, though, in linguistics, literature, and ethnopoetics, have brought us to the stage where such comparative and developmental analysis of spoken narratives can be attempted with considerably greater confidence than heretofore (as in Hymes 1985).

On the premise that continuity and change are rooted most fundamentally in the storytelling practice of individual narrators across changing contexts, this chapter is offered as a beginning attempt to help fill the gap I have noted. It is an examination of the changes in a limited range of one storyteller's narration as the contexts of his storytelling have shifted over time.

Ed Bell, storyteller

Ed Bell, of Luling, Texas, is a masterful storyteller who has gained increasing celebrity over the past decade as the subject of several scholarly essays, appearances at national, regional, and local folk festivals, a number of feature articles in newspapers and magazines, and even a recent appearance on a network television show. He was born on his father's ranch at the headwaters of the Frio River, in 1905, but his family shifted residence several times during his childhood, settling eventually in Caldwell County, between Luling and Lockhart. Bell attributes his penchant for storytelling in part to the mobility of his family during his boyhood; he cultivated his verbal ability as a way of gaining entree into the established peer groups of each new locale into which his family moved. Still another formative factor that he identifies is the experience of listening to and telling stories with friends around campfires while out hunting during his teenage years in Caldwell County.

The great flowering of his talents as a storyteller, though, occurred during his four decades as proprietor of a fishing camp in Indianola, on the Texas Gulf Coast, where he had moved during the Depression. Indeed, he attributes a portion of his success in running the fishing camp to his abilities as a raconteur, which helped keep visitors coming back year after year and attracted new clients as well (cf. Cothran 1974:341).

In 1967, when folklorist Pat Mullen was doing field research on the folklore of the Texas Gulf Coast, Ed Bell's renown as a storyteller extended up and down the coast from Indianola for miles in either direction. Mullen visited Bell at his fishing camp on two occasions, in 1967, and 1971, and recorded a number of his stories of various kinds, including treasure tales, tales of local characters, legends, and tall tales, under conditions "close to the natural context of the usual storytelling events" (Mullen 1978:133; see also Mullen 1976). In 1972, Bell retired from the fishing camp to his family's place near Luling, where Mullen recorded him again in 1975, in preparation for his participation in the Smithsonian Festival of American Folklife the following year. Still more recordings were made during the Festival itself. On his later visits, Mullen taped successive tellings of a number of Bell's stories originally recorded in 1967, as well as much contextual information concerning Bell's life history and career, performance style, and sense of his art. On the basis of this information, Mullen was able to document and analyze certain developmental changes in Ed Bell's storytelling over the intervals between 1967–71 and 1971–5 (Mullen 1978:130–48, 1981). I will have occasion to discuss his findings in more detail later.

In a later essay (1981), Mullen went on to discuss further changes in Ed Bell's storytelling at the point where he had just begun to perform at folk festivals, before clubs, and in other public settings. Mullen analyzes in this study the beginning of Bell's recasting of his repertoire, his growing self-consciousness about the nature of performance, and his developing assessment of the new situational factors bearing on his performance in these new contexts. This is an important essay, perhaps the first scholarly, analytical study of the effect on a traditional storyteller of a shift from local, intimate, small-scale performance contexts to large-scale public folk festivals, and I shall draw upon its findings as well.

Documentation of Ed Bell continued in 1979, when Pat Jasper, then Humanist in Residence at the public-access cable television station in Austin, made him the subject of one of four programs documenting the folk traditions of Central Texas. Her videotape recordings include some stories recorded earlier by Mullen, thereby adding further to the comparative record (Jasper 1979). More recently, I have recorded Bell on several occasions during 1982–3 at our respective homes, the University of Texas, and the Texas Folklife Festival in San Antonio, again requesting some of the same stories recorded over the years by Mullen and Jasper. All told, then, we have a documentary record of Ed Bell's storytelling that spans more than 15 years, including multiple tellings of a number of stories.

Mullen's writings trace certain changes in Ed Bell's storytelling up to the point when he had newly embarked upon his career as a public performer, in 1976. These changes include a very early shift away from occasional third-person narration in some of his tall tales to full first-person narration (Mullen 1978:140–5). In the years since then, further changes have taken place as Bell has continued and developed his activities as a public storyteller, and I propose in this chapter to trace important aspects of that change. My analysis will build upon Mullen's revealing work, but will depart from it in certain respects. Whereas one of Mullen's principal concerns was to trace Bell's shifts in repertoire for the new performance situations in which he found himself and the new audiences he found there, I will focus on changes over time in stories that have persisted in his repertoire, stories that he has continued to tell from the years at the fishing camp up to the present. I will look more closely at the stylistic devices that account for the textual differences between the first recorded tellings – in 1967 and 1971 – and the most recent ones, and I will attempt to relate those changes to the changing circumstances surrounding Ed Bell's performances.

On first examination of the transcribed texts of the stories for which we have both early and more recent tellings, perhaps the most immediately apparent difference between them is the considerably greater length of the latter. For example, Mullen has published two versions of Ed Bell's tall tale, "Redfishing in a Fog Bank" (called "The Thick Fog" in Mullen's book; 1978:139–40), one dating from 1967 and one from 1971. The texts of these stories in Mullen's transcription run to 395 and 414 words, respectively. I have included in the Appendix to this chapter a transcription of this same tale as told in 1982. The text contains 681 words, making it 72 percent longer than the 1967 telling and 64 percent longer than the 1971 version. Likewise, the 1982 telling of "The Wonderful Hunt" also given in the Appendix is 82 percent longer than the text recorded by Mullen in 1967 and 75 percent longer than the 1971 telling (Mullen 1978:141–3), based on a simple word count.

Ed Bell himself is quite cognizant of this trend toward lengthening in his tales. In reply to a query about the nature of the changes in his stories since he left the fishing camp and began performing at festivals, he stated that "there have been quite a few changes in lots of the stories, but most of the changes have really been additions. [. . .] I usually add something to my stories" (cf. Dégh 1969:224, 240).

Increased length, of course, is a rather gross measure of narrative change. I propose in what follows to specify more precisely the nature and patterning of the differences between the early and late tellings that make for the far greater length of the latter. I will focus on Ed Bell's tall tales, since these are the showpieces of his repertoire and the best-documented of his stories over time. My examples will be drawn from three tellings of "The Bee Tree," one recorded by Mullen in 1971 at the fishing camp, one recorded by Jasper in 1979 at Bell's home, and the last recorded by myself in 1982 at the University of Texas. The changes in "The Bee Tree," however, are quite representative;

the same factors may be seen at work in "Redfishing in a Fog Bank" and "The Wonderful Hunt," and characterize Bell's entire tall tale repertoire. Here are the texts:[1]

The Bee Tree (1971)
Orientation
No, that happened, though, up near Luling. We had pretty good woods up in there, and some of the trees were big.

1
But I staggered up on a tree one day that I didn't believe. I couldn't believe my eyes. I couldn't – it just looked like the tree took up nearly the whole country. And I heard a terrific roar, and I looked up, and about forty feet high was a big old knothole about a foot across, and was a solid roll of bees just working out and in there, honey bees. So, man, I just knew that I'd get a big bunch of honey out of that.

2
So I went off and rounded up a bunch of my friends; we got about ten of us with axes. We loaded up the wagon with all the tubs and old barrels, dishpans, everything we could find because we didn't know how much honey we might get out of it. We went down there with our camp outfit too. We was going to camp there while we chopped it down.

3
So we chopped on it three days, and the old boy says, "You know, I can hear something that sounds like an echo of us chopping on this tree." I says, "You know, I've never been on the other side of that tree. I'm going to walk around there and see what it is."

4
Why, it took quite a while to walk around it. Got over there and there was ten other fellows chopping on the other side. They'd found the bee tree too.

5
So we all lit in together, decided to pool our chopping and get it down. So we all got busy, and we chopped the tree down and a big branch [stream] there about twenty-five foot deep, around a hundred feet across, pretty steep sides on it. And this tree fell across that, and

---

[1] Type 1960G The Great Tree. Motifs H86 Inscribed name on article as token of ownership; X1116 The breathing tree; X1471 Lie about large trees; X1471.1 Two men or gangs of men chop on opposite sides of big tree, each unaware that anyone is working on other side; X1547.2 Lie: river of honey (Baughman 1966; Thompson 1955–8). For another version of "The Bee Tree" as told by Ed Bell, see Sitton (1983:166–8).

it just busted open, and a big limb broke open at the same time, and there was squirrels in that limb, and a roll of gray squirrels big as a flour barrel rolled out of that hollow limb for three days and nights. I don't know where they all went to after that, but there sure was a lot of squirrels in there. So we looked, and this tree was split open and turned over into halves, and there was small knotholes on the sides of it; in different places, but they's there. So there's just streams of honey coming out of there, so we told that other bunch that they could catch out of one stream and we'd catch out of the other. And we filled everything we had, all the barrels, dishpans, tubs, and everything we could find we filled with honey. And it was still running out of there. And these other guys didn't have near as much as we did to catch honey with.

6

So we took off. They went one direction, and the way we went we had to cross this branch [stream] about five miles further down. We got there, and it hadn't rained in six months, and that thing was bank full. And we wondered what in the world had happened, and we got up there and looked at it, and it was pure honey running down that branch. It's done filled that branch plumb full. We had to wait two days for it to run down so we could cross and get home. (Mullen 1978:145–6; paragraphing and numbering of episodes added)

The Bee Tree (1979)
Orientation
When I was a lot younger than I am now, fact a whole lot younger, why I used to like to go possum huntin' them pretty days, especially after a norther. And I'd very often get my ax or my .22 and go out in the woods, and this day I took my kind of little hand ax. I walked off down the woods and checkin' on hollow trees, 'cause those possums'd den up in hollow trees. If I got a possum why that meant about 30 cents for 'is skin. I like to hunt for fur and such as that 'cause I like to spend that money too.

Well one day I was way down southeast of the house 'bout three miles, and I'd been tired of climbin' big trees anyway, and I was just huntin' for little trees to climb. 'Bout to run out of hollow trees.

1

So I stepped over on the other side of Rock Water Hole Branch. Rock Water Hole Branch was about ten foot deep, and forty, fifty feet wide. And it was a dry branch. It don't no water run down at all unless it's just rained lately. So, I walked over on the other side and lookin' at some trees there, and I couldn' believe my eyes! Right there was a tree that was bigger than anything that I'd ever seen or ever dreamed of. That tree was a monster. It was great big ol' tree, big, big.

And I don't blame y'all if you don't believe me about this tree, because I wouldn't believe it either if I hadn'ta seen it with my own eyes. I don' know whether I can tell ya how you could believe it or not, but that was a big tree. And I was standin' there admirin' it, and I looked up, and my mouth opened, I guess, 'cause I . . . I tell you I's astonished. And when I threw my head way back and looked up there, there was a roll of bees comin' out of a hole up there about ten inches, 'bout that big. And there's a solid mass of bees goin' out and in there. Just a roarin' sound. Oh my goodness, that was a bee tree out of this world! And I figured, no tellin' how much honey was in there.

Right, well, shoot, I better mark that thing. I put my brand on it. You know, we all put a X on a bee tree, for a brand. Which is pretty good idea, to brand anything, you know, to kinda own it. It's ownership. I put the X on there, and right down below that X, I put E.B., just chopped it out with my ax. And, that was my bee tree. Sure it was, I was sure of it.

2

I come on back to the house, see my daddy. See if he wouldn't let me go down there and cut it. So, yes sir, daddy would let me do it. But he didn't like the idea much. He said, "Buddy," he said, "you got, uh, you got the foolishest notions I ever heard of." Say, "Your imagination just runs wild with you."

Well, well, O.K. So, I says, "I sure would like to go cut that bee tree, though, papa. I could get Parm Williams, and Alec Moore, and we'd go down there and cut that bee tree. It might take us two or three, four days."

Papa says, "Well Buddy, I won't need the wagon and team for several days, but you better get your ma to put you up some sandwiches, and maybe some pinto beans and salt pork to cook, 'cause y'all gon' be gone that long you'll sure need somethin' to eat." He's kinda jokin' me. But I did.

3

I got everything ready like that, and got Parm and Alec over there and Parm and Alec was laughin' at me, because they just figured I was just jokin'. Tryin' to get papa to let me have a wagon so we'd have a kind of a picnic out there ya know. So we got everything loaded, and they even went along with gettin' these buckets and barrels. Dishpans. Everything, even fruit jars, that we could find to put honey in. They even went along with me on that. We got all that stuff loaded.

4

Well from the house going down to where that bee tree was, Rock Water Hole Branch makes a great big bend, a big bend. Well, if you . . . you can cross Rock Water Hole twice, between the house and that place. And it's only about three miles. If you have to go around that bend it's about three miles further. Makes it pretty far in a wagon and team. So, we started off down there. We just crossed that Water Hole Branch, see. First time, the second time, we were pretty close to the bee tree then. Hove over there, and we put the . . . we stopped for a camp way out from that tree, because those boys never had seen that tree. Nobody else as far as I know had ever seen that tree in that whole country. 'Cause it was astonishingly big, everybody would've known about it if anybody'd seen it. So we went over there and looked at that and decided to eat 'fore we went to choppin' on it.

5

And right after dinner, after we'd eat some of those sandwiches, we got over there and we just went to cuttin' on that tree. We just cut like the dickens.

6

And we'd been choppin' about two days and I decided I could hear some peckin' on the other side. Well those boys knew that I was kinda lazy, but I told them anyway that I'd like to just go around the tree and see what that peckin' noise was. Well they was kind of curious about that peckin' noise too. And they said, "Go ahead Ed." Says, "We know you're tryin' to pook off some, just because you was the one that found the tree. I guess you got a right to pook off a little bit."

Well, I walked around that tree and it was a long ways around there. But when I got past the middle of it, going down the other side, I believed I could see somebody down there and it sounded just like they was choppin' on that tree. Well, I got to feelin' awful bad, 'cause, man somebody's cuttin' my bee tree, I didn't like it one bit.

7

Sure enough, I got down there where they was and there was three boys over there. And they'd been choppin' two or three days on that tree. And I said "Say fellas, y'all stealin' my bee tree?"

Well they knew me and they said, "No, Ed," said "we're not stealin' your bee tree. This is our bee tree."

Well, they showed me their X over there and one ol' boy had his initials under the X. Well, we, uh, we didn't know which one had found it and marked it first, 'cause the other boys marked it the same day I did.

Well, I said, "Let's just chop it down and divide the honey."

Oh, they just thought that was real fine. That was all right by them.

8

So I went back around there and then told Parm and Alec what had happened. We started in, all three choppin' on that, and I didn't mind choppin' then 'cause there's some other fellas helpin' us.

9

Well it took us about five days to chop that darn tree down, 'cause it was a whopper. We finally got it down. And when that thing fell, we could tell it was gon' fall our way because we was next to Rock Water Hole Branch. Folks, we sure did have to run to get out of the way of that tree, because it was a long way out the side of it. We run like heck when it first started crackin'.

Well it fell across the branch. And there was a great big ol' limb broke off, about, oh, about this big around [makes circle with his fingers]. And this roll of gray squirrels come out of that limb for three days and nights. We got all the squirrel we could eat there offa those three days and nights while we was gathering up the honey.

Well, we just gathered honey and we gathred honey. Filled up all those buckets. We filled up all those barrels. We filled the tubs too. The dishpan. And the fruit jars. We just filled them all with honey. There was a great big ol' place there, pourin' out of the side of the tree, about that big [makes circle with his fingers], just a . . . just spewin' out like that and down into Rock Water Hole Branch

Well I'd never seen anything like it and the other boys didn't either. But those other boys cheated on us. They . . . they had more vessels to put the honey in than we did. So I think they got about a gallon more honey than we did. But I guess it was all right 'cause we had more honey than we'd ever eat anyway. And then we might come back down get some out of the branch if we just wanted some more honey.

10

We got everything rigged up and we started in. Well we went up to that crossin' of that Rock Water Hole Branch. It's level brim full! Ain't rained in a month. Alec jumped out and went over and looked at it. He said, "That's right Ed, it's pure honey. Nothin' in the world but just honey."

And I . . . "Well, I'll be darned, that much of it – wait a minute. This is the wrong way. This is runnin' uphill!"

"Well I can't do nothin' about that."

So we gotta go the long way around home. We went around that way, plum around that big bend, and we had to go right by the other crossin'. Well, we went right by it and we checked that Rock Water Hole Branch and it was still level full up there. And that's about three miles o' creek up there to where it got halfway on account of such a big bend.

11

And when we, uh, last time we looked at that creek, why it was still level full o' honey. And I imagine it's still runnin' level full of honey.

The Bee Tree (1982)

Orientation

You know, folks, over at, uh, near Luling, Texas where I come from, uh, there's, we got woods out there, big lots and lots o' woods, but not very many big trees. A tree that's three feet in diameter's a big tree. It's sure big.

One year I was huntin' possums or something, and uh, off down on Rock Water Hole Branch. That was about two miles below our place and it's a dry branch, it just . . . it doesn't run any water or anything.

1

Well, I looked over across that branch and I saw the biggest tree I've ever seen in my life. You've heard o' those big ol', uh, trees in California, you know, bein' so big. Well this tree was so big couldn't even see either side of it. Course it was kinda hid with brush too. And I stared at that tree and I looked all around. Well I couldn't believe that a tree was that big would be down there. Never had seen it. Sure hadn't. And while I was lookin' up to see the heighth of it, I could see something moving up there [looks up]. That's bees. That's bees goin' out and in! Folks, there was a place about six inches across, a little knothole and the bees were just swarmin' through that hole, just ZZZzzzzzzzzzzz.

Well, you know I was really intrigued by that bein' a bee tree. I thought, you know I'd like to get that honey. That's what I always think of, get some honey, you know, or get whatever's there to be gotten.

2

So I went home and asked papa if I could take the wagon, team, go down there and chop that bee tree down.

He said, "Buddy, you got the strongest imagination of anybody I ever heard tell of." He said, "you know there's not any tree that big down there, and if it is that big you couldn't cut it down."

I says, "Papa, I'll get Alec Moore and Parm Williams to go down and help me."

3

So Alec and Parm promised to go and dad said, "Well, you can take the wagon team, I won't need 'em this week. How long you gon' stay?"

I says, "Papa, it's gon' take several days to chop that tree down."
So he says, "Better get your mama to fix some food."

Well, mama's done fixed it. She heard about me gon' be gone three or four days, and I was Buddy, I'm the oldest boy. And you know it's a funny thing with these women, really think their oldest boy is somethin' special, whether he is or not.

4

Anyway, I went down there to chop this tree, takin' the beans mama'd cooked and the biscuits she'd baked, and Parm, and Alec. We got down to Rock Water Hole Branch. And by the way, while you're goin' down there from the house, you have to cross this branch twice. Or, you've got to go about two miles around the big bend. Well, why go that bend? We just cut across and it was two miles down there.

5

We got down there and those boys was . . . were enthralled. I'm tellin' you, they couldn't believe it. They said, "Ed, we've been here for years and we've never seen that tree. We still don't believe it's a bee tree."

I said, "Well, I don't either. We're all even."

So we got off over there and we looked that tree over. Yup, it's a bee tree. And there's my mark, big ol' X on there, and E.B. right under it. Well, that made it legal.

So we went on back, unhitched that team, put 'em away out there, way off from the place, so the tree wouldn't fall on 'em when we got it chopped down. Course we was thinkin' about choppin' it down right quick.

6

We started choppin' on that tree, and we hadn't been cuttin' very long, until I got kinda tired. I stopped, I listened, I hear a "chop, chop, chop." Now my goodness. That's . . . I believe that's somebody choppin' on the other side.

Oh man, my hackles raised right quick and I was gonna see what's wrong. So I told those boys, I said, "Listen, if y'all don't mind I'm goin' on the other side'n see, I believe there's somebody choppin' on the other side o' this tree."

Well Parm says, "Go ahead, Ed, you done all the findin' o' the tree, so we'll just keep on choppin'."

7

Well I went 'round the side o' that tree and back on the other side, and there's three o' those ol' Harwood boys, they'd found this tree and they was choppin' on the other side.

Well, we had a little argument at first, but they showed me there was their mark right up there on that bee tree. That made it legal. So I said, "Listen, let's just all cut it down and divide the honey."

"O.K., that's fine."

8

Went back and went to choppin'. We chopped for two or three days, and every once in a while I'd look up at that hole, them bees swarmin' out and in. And I got to noticin' one o' those limbs up there kinda swellin' and settlin' back down. I said, "What in the world's the matter with that? Never saw a tree do that." Well, I dismissed it, just a crazy tree anyhow.

9

Went ahead choppin', finally we got that thing cut down. I think it was about five days we chopped on that thing. And it fell right across Rock Water Hole Branch. And it was about ten foot deep and that made the hole up above the Branch quite a piece and one o' the limbs broke open down there just about four inches wide, just below where the bees went in, and do you know they's just a solid stream o' honey started runnin' out o' that thing?

Well, we was all excited over that and one of 'em hollered then and says, "Look, look, look." Great big ol' limb about three feet in diameter'd broke off, and that was the limb that had been givin' it out and in, kinda like a bellows, and there's a row o' gray squirrels come outa that limb for three days and nights. There'd been so many in there every time they took a deep breath they'd swell the limb up.

Well, we had the gray squirrel t'eat, we had beans, and we had biscuits, and we was fillin' up all of our vessels. We brought tubs, buckets, fruit jars, pitchers, everything we could find we brought along with us to put that honey in.

Those other boys had too. They was camped way over on the other side o' the Branch, the other side o' where the tree was at. So, we was all fillin' up. I didn't kinda like it 'cause those other boys had more vessels really than we did, and they got more honey'n us. I really thought I found the tree first.

But anyway, why we's gettin' all this honey gathered up, we got all the squirrels we could eat, why we couldn't stand to eat a squirrel any more. So we decided to go home.

That honey, now folks, was still pourin' outa that six-inch hole,

into Rock Water Hole Branch. And it was just f-f-f-fooooo in there, like that [flowing gesture].
10
Well, we got in this old wagon, hitched the team up; got in the wagon, started out home. We got to the first crossin' of Rock Water Hole Branch and it looked like it was level full. I . . . Well, what in the world? It hadn't rained in weeks.

Parm jumped out and run over there and he hollered, "Ed, it's honey. It's full o' honey!"

Well, I couldn't, uh . . . uh, couldn't believe that, but I . . . it had to be. And we went on two miles around now, three, whatever it was – it was a long ways. We got up to the other crossin' and it was full o' honey too.

Now folks, this was *upstream* from where we cut that bee tree. It wasn't downstream, it was upstream.
Coda
And folks, as far as I know that creek is still runnin' bank full with honey.

Expansion of plot

Proliferation of episodes

Let us look first at changes in the story plot. On first examination, it may appear that the plot has changed very little from the early to the later tellings. The main episodes of the 1971 version are as follows:

1. The discovery of the bee tree
2. The organization of the expedition to chop it down and gather the honey
3. The chopping of the tree
4. The encounter with the other party of choppers
5. The felling of the tree and the gathering of the honey
6. The return home

All are preserved, in the same sequence, in the two later versions. The most apparent change in plot is the addition in both later tellings of the episode recounting the encounter between Ed Bell and his father, in which he asks permission to go off and cut down the tree. As we shall see, this episode is introduced more for metanarrational purposes than for its contribution to the developmental unfolding of the narrative.

If we refine our conception of narrative plot, however, this dimension of change takes on a clearer and more complex aspect. First, we must be more precise about what we mean by episode. For present purposes, I will take episodes to be major segments of the narrative plot constituted by time junctures. That is, whereas the flow of the narrative discourse is continuous, the events of the plot may be reported discontinuously, set off from each other by intervals of elapsed time that go unreported in the narrative; that is what Genette (1980:51) calls *ellipsis,* a break in the temporal continuity of the narrative. Within each episode, the flow of narrative time is uninterrupted, although not necessarily constant in rate. Episodes are often – but not always – marked off initially in these narratives by initial particles: "well," "so," "anyway." The episodes that constitute the plot are preceded by an orientation section, which is not an episode insofar as it does not report any of the narrative action but rather sets the stage for it by locating the narrated events in time and space (Labov and Waletzky 1967:32; Chafe 1980a:42; Colby 1973:654). In the two later versions, the narrative is concluded by a coda, likewise not an episode, but serving rather to bridge the gap between story time and the present, that is, the time of the narrated event and the time of the telling (Labov and Waletzky 1967:33–40).

The 1971 version of "The Bee Tree," as noted, is made up of six episodes preceded by an orientation. In the two later tellings, the number of episodes has increased to ten and a coda has been added. Table 1 sets out the sequence of episodes in each text in such a way as to indicate correspondences and differences across the three. Note that the proliferation of episodes does not alter in any way the sequence of episodes established in the 1971 telling, nor are any of the original six episodes eliminated in the later texts. All the changes are additive. As Ed Bell puts it himself, "You know, the main framework of a story goes along just the same," and "It's easier to add on a part of a story than it is to change up the complex of it."

As Table 1 demonstrates, all three versions begin with an orientation and the episode recounting the discovery of the bee tree. Whereas the earliest version then proceeds to the preparations for going out to cut the tree, the two later tellings interject a new episode in which Ed Bell asks his father's permission to cut the tree before going on to the organization of the expedition to do so. The new episode may be seen as an elaboration of the account of preparations for cutting the tree and does little, if anything, to advance the action of the narrative. As I have suggested, though, this episode carries a heavy metanarrational load, and I will deal with it in more detail later in the chapter.

The second slot in which new episodes are added occurs after the preparations to cut the tree, common to all three versions. Between this episode and the one recounting the first stint of chopping, the 1979 version introduces an episode recounting the trip that Bell and his companions took out to the tree, to which the 1982 version adds still another episode describing their arrival at the tree.

On examination, we may see that these new episodes are accommodated into the narrative by taking advantage of the structural opportunity afforded

Table 1. *Episodes in the three tellings of "The Bee Tree" by Ed Bell*

1971	1979	1982
Orientation	Orientation	Orientation
Discovery of tree	Discovery of tree	Discovery of tree
–	Asking father's permission to cut tree	Asking father's permission to cut tree
Preparations to cut tree	Preparations to cut tree	Preparations to cut tree
–	Trip out to tree	Trip out to tree
–	–	Arrival at tree
First stint of chopping and hearing noise	First stint of chopping	First stint of chopping and hearing noise
–	Hearing other choppers and setting off to locate source of noise	–
Encounter with other choppers	Encounter with other choppers	Encounter with other choppers
–	Return to first side of tree and recommencement of chopping	Return to first side of tree and recommencement of chopping
Felling tree and gathering honey	Felling tree and gathering honey	Felling tree and gathering honey
Return home	Return home	Return home
–	Coda	Coda

by the ellipsis between episodes already established in the first telling. That is, they present information that fits into the time interval between the organization of the expedition to cut the tree and the commencement of the actual chopping. Since in the earliest text these two episodes are set in different places, the new episode(s) are appropriately accounts of movement from one significant scene to the next. The later episode, in which Bell returns to the first side of the tree from his encounter with the other party of choppers, exploits the same structural potential by recounting movement from one scene to another, information omitted in the first telling.

I do not mean to suggest by these observations that these new episodes are mere filler, without significant function in their respective texts. Indeed, the episode recounting the trip out to the tree in both later texts contributes effectively to the formal structure of the story. It establishes an episode to stand in parallel to the final one, the return home, and by establishing the crossing of Rock Water Hole Branch as potentially problematic it foreshadows the necessity of taking the long way home when the creek is full of honey, thus enhancing the cohesion of the narrative. Likewise, the additional episode about the arrival at the tree stands in parallel to the first one, the discovery of the tree by Bell, in that it matches his initial incredulity with his friends' similar reaction. I will come back to this structural factor later in the discussion.

Beyond the interposition of transitional episodes, a further device by which episodes may be proliferated is illustrated by the 1979 version of "The Bee Tree," in which the narrator makes two episodes of what is treated in a single one in the 1971 and 1982 texts. This involves separating the first stint of chopping from the hearing of the other party of choppers and Bell's setting off to locate the source of the noise. In all three texts, the action of chopping is durative, consistent with the immensity of the tree, but in the first version the hearing of the other choppers occurs while Bell and his friends are themselves at work on their own side of the tree, with no break in the action, whereas in the 1982 text, Bell gets tired, stops to rest, and immediately hears the noise of the other party. Durative action, though, offers the potential of being narratively broken; the narrative account of such continued action may be suspended while the action is in progress, to be resumed at a later point antecedent to the next reported action, thereby providing an ellipsis that sets off two episodes. This is what happens in the 1979 text:

> And right after dinner, after we'd eat some of those sandwiches, we got over there and we just went to cuttin' on that tree. We just cut like the dickens.
> And we'd been choppin' about two days and I decided I could hear some peckin' on the other side.

The result is two episodes in place of one.

The final addition to the two longer texts, as noted, is a coda, which effects a transition between the narrated event and the narrative event. Although a coda is not necessary for narrative closure – the 1971 version stands quite well without one – it does enhance the performative efficacy of the narration by seeming to confirm the truth of the tale: Rock Water Hole Branch was still flowing level full of honey a short while ago, so perhaps it still is. The coda thus complements much of the metanarrational discourse, which also colors these later versions. I will deal with this dimension of the stories in a later section.

Thus, to summarize the means by which Ed Bell has expanded his telling of "The Bee Tree," we have discovered the following devices:

1. The addition of a metanarrational episode (to be treated in a later section)
2. The interposition of transitional episodes in the previously unfilled time intervals between established episodes
3. The splitting of a single episode into two by suspending and then resuming durative action
4. The addition of a narrative coda

Addition of new motifs

Episodes are macrounits of narrative plot. Having demonstrated the proliferation of episodes in the later versions of "The Bee Tree" as told by Ed Bell, we may proceed to an examination of other means by which he expands the content of the stories.

One mechanism, familiar to folklorists, is the incorporation of additional narrative motifs, traditional elements of narrative content. We do not find this often in Bell's tales, because it is in the nature of traditional motifs that they have "something striking or unusual" about them (Thompson 1946:415), and they therefore have the capacity to "change up the complex" of the tale more than Bell is inclined to allow; as I have noted, his plots do not tend to change over time. There is, nevertheless, one new motif in the 1979 version of "The Bee Tree," namely, the branding of the tree to indicate ownership (H 86 Inscribed name on article as token of ownership). This motif appears also in the 1982 version, together with a second new motif, the limb that expands and contracts with the breathing of the squirrels packed so densely inside it (X1116 The breathing tree).

As regards the branding of the tree motif in the two later versions of the tale, we may note that the first telling already includes the assertion of Bell's claim to the tree against that of the party of choppers he discovers on the other side. The branding of the tree in the later tellings thus explains and elaborates this plot element by specifying the customary method of establishing a claim to a honey tree.

The swelling limb motif is a very common one in American tall tales about hunting (X1116 The breathing tree) and has been familiar to Bell since his youth. The inclusion of this motif does not alter the contour of the story, because the great mass of squirrels was present in his telling from the first. The swelling limb is not so much a new element in the plot as an elaboration of an element of content already included in the story. And once having introduced the swelling limb in the second chopping episode, it makes for still further expansion of the tale when the tree is felled and the limb bursts open, for the connection between the squirrels that pour out of the tree and the peculiar limb calls for an explanation: "There'd been so many in there every time they took a deep breath they'd swell the limb up."

Formal devices

Beyond the level of content, there are other means, perhaps more important, by which Ed Bell elaborates elements of "The Bee Tree" in the later tellings. These involve the exploitation of an interesting range of formal devices, including especially direct discourse and parallelism. We may illustrate the use and effects of these devices by comparing equivalent episodes across all three tellings of the tale; let us look for our first examples at the episode of the encounter with the other party of choppers. To facilitate comparison in this regard, I have set the relevant passages out into lines defined prosodically by pauses (Tedlock 1972a), corresponding also to clause or sentence boundaries. Not every clause marks a line break, but every new line begins a new clause or sentence. The passage from the 1971 version includes one sentence from the succeeding episode, which contains information presented in the encounter episode in the two later texts.

1971
Well, it took quite a while to walk around it.
Got over there
And there was ten other fellows choppin' on the other side.
They'd found the bee tree too.

So we all lit in together,
decided to pool our choppin' and get it down.

1979
Sure enough, I got down there where they was
and there was three boys over there.
And they'd been choppin' two or three days on that tree.
And I said, ''Say, fellas, y'all stealin' my bee tree?''
Well, they knew me
And they said, ''No, Ed,'' said, ''we're not stealin' your bee tree.
This is our bee tree.''
Well, they showed me their X over there
and one ol' boy had his initials under the X.
Well, we uh,
we didn't know which one had found it and marked it first,
'cause the other boys marked it the same day I did.
Well, I said, ''Let's just chop it down and divide the honey.''
Oh, they just thought that was real fine.
That was all right by them.

1982
Well, I went away 'round the other side o' that tree and back on the
     other side,
and there's three o' those ol' Harwood boys,
they'd found this tree and they was choppin' on the other side.
Well, we had a little argument at first,
but they showed me there was their mark right up there on that bee
     tree.
That made it legal.
So I said, ''listen, let's just all cut it down and divide the honey.''
''O.K., that's fine.''

Direct discourse

The first passage, from the 1971 telling, is notably lean. The discourse is a straightforward and economical narrative account of Bell's walk to the other side of the tree, his discovery of the other party of choppers who were also after the honey, and the pooling of their efforts to fell the tree.

As regards the two later accounts, we have already noted the matter of the branding of the tree, in parallel to Bell's own marking of it. But consider now the management of the discourse. In the earliest version, the negotiation of the competing claims to the tree is not recounted at all; the upshot of the encounter is simply summarized by "decided to pool our choppin' and get it down." In the later versions, by contrast, the interaction is recounted, with parts of it, in effect, being reenacted through direct discourse. The passage in the 1982 version includes one exchange of quoted speech, consisting of two turns at talk, whereas the 1979 version is the fullest of all, incorporating two exchanges, one of two turns at talk, the other one turn, with other aspects of the narration reported more summarily.

The increased resort to direct discourse reaches beyond this one episode; it may be seen to operate throughout both of the later texts. In the 1971 version of "The Bee Tree" we find only a single exchange of quoted speech, in the episode in which Bell and his friends hear chopping on the other side of the tree and agree that he should investigate. In fact, direct discourse is employed in this episode in all three versions. In the later texts, beyond the quoted speech in this episode and the one recounting Bell's encounter with the other choppers that we have already examined, we also find instances of quoted speech in the new episodes, including the exchange between Bell and his father, in which he asks permission to cut the tree (1979 and 1982) and the arrival at the tree (1982), and one bit of quoted interior speech when he spies the swelling limb (1982), all of which we have already identified as expansions of the tale. The remaining instances are to be found in episodes present in all three texts but amplified by direct discourse only in the later ones: the cry, "Look, look, look," as the squirrels pour out of the felled tree (1982), and the expressions of surprise at finding Rock Water Hole Branch filled to the banks with honey on the return home (1979 and 1982). In all, there are ten quoted utterances in the 1979 text and fourteen in the 1982 text, whereas there are only two in 1971. Direct discourse clearly represents a significant stylistic resource for the expansion of the later texts.

Syntactic parallelism

Parallelism is repetition with systematic variation, the combining of variant and invariant elements in the construction of a poetic work (Fox 1977; Jakobson 1966, 1968). Parallel structures may be developed at a range of formal levels: phonological, prosodic, syntactic, semantic, thematic. Most significant in Ed Bell's expansion of his tales are syntactic and thematic parallelism.

Bell employs syntactic parallelism in a variety of ways in his stories. For example, the dialogue between Bell and the other party of choppers in the 1979 text quoted above is organized in terms of parallel lines:

> And I said, "Say, fellas, y'all stealin' my bee tree?"
> Well, they knew me
> and they said, "No, Ed," said, "we're not stealin' your bee tree.
> This is our bee tree."

Here, the element of variation, effected by the operation of negation and pronoun shifts ("we're *not* stealin' *your* bee tree. This is *our* bee tree") offsets the redundancy of the repeated elements in the unfolding of the exchange by presenting new information that advances the line of the narrative.

But consider the lines that close the episode in this same text:

> Oh, they thought that was real fine.
> That was all right by them.

This is a far more redundant pairing, effectively a paraphrase, in which the second line restates the central meaning of the preceding one in different words; either line alone would suffice. Redundant, paraphrastic parallel constructions of this kind contribute perceptibly to the expansion of the later texts; examples are abundant and readily apparent. I will here cite only a few, selected from the opening episode of the 1982 text, to make the point that the redundant parallel constructions are employed for a full range of narrative functions. Thus we find statements of action ("And I stared at that tree and I looked all around"), description ("That's bees. That's bees goin' out and in . . . and the bees were just swarmin' through that hole"), and metanarration ("I thought, you know, I'd like to get that honey. That's what I always think of, get some honey, you know") constructed in parallel and paraphrase.

Thematic parallelism

Parallelism is not confined in the later tellings to the language of the narration (see our earlier discussion of the proliferation of episodes and the introduction of other new content). Indeed, thematic parallelism – repetition with systematic variation of an element of plot, from simple action to entire episode – reveals itself as a major structural device in the overall construction of the story line of the two later texts (cf. Jakobson and Pomorska 1983:106–7). This constructional pattern is already in evidence, to be sure, in the earliest telling, in the introduction of the second party of choppers, whose discovery and chopping of the tree parallel Bell's own and help to underscore the enormousness of the tree. The later texts, however, are marked by a proliferation of parallel plot elements in Bell's elaboration of the story. From the vantage point of the 1971 text, the paired elements may be seen to be established in two ways in the 1979 and 1982 versions.

One device builds on content elements originally present in the 1971 version by inserting elements parallel to them in the later expansion of the narrative. We have seen, for instance, that the episode recounting the trip of Bell and his friends out to the bee tree, included in both later versions, sets up a chiastic parallel with the final episode recounting the trip home, present in all three tellings. In the former, going out to the tree, Bell makes the point that the boys can easily cross Rock Water Hole Branch when it is dry, foreshadowing the problem they encounter on the trip back home when the creek is bank-full of honey. Here an element of content is inserted early in the story to establish a parallel with one already present at the end. By contrast, Bell's incredulity at the great size of the bee tree, of which much is made at the beginning of all three versions, is paired in the 1982 version with the later expression of disbelief by his friends when they first see the tree. Both cases add an element – episode or action – in the later tellings in order to establish a pair with one already present in the first one. In other cases, both parts of the set of parallel elements are included for the first time in the expanded versions. A case in point that we have already noted is the complementary pair of brands carved into the tree by Bell and the other party of choppers. Either way, by the doubling of existing elements or by the insertion of new pairs of parallel elements, Bell is able to use the structural device of thematic parallelism to expand the plot of his narratives (cf. Finnegan 1967:90).

Metanarration

At several points in the foregoing discussion of the means and devices by which Ed Bell expands his narratives in the later tellings, I have had occasion to mention metanarration in passing, deferring explicit consideration of it to a later point in the discussion. I turn now to an analysis of this prominent dimension of Bell's storytelling.

By metanarration, I mean those devices that index or comment on the narrative itself (such as its message, generic form and function, and discourse) or on the components or conduct of the storytelling event (including participants, organization, and action) (Babcock 1977). Strictly speaking, there is no narration without metanarration, but I will reserve consideration here for those aspects of Bell's storytelling discourse in which the metanarrational function becomes overt or sufficiently prominent to call attention to itself.

Consider first explicitly metanarrational discourse. The 1971 text, significantly, is entirely without such overt metanarration, contrasting markedly in this respect with the two later ones. Overtly metanarrational statements represent shifts in the alignment Bell takes to himself and others present as expressed in the way he manages the production of his discourse in the course of telling the story (Goffman 1981:128). They are shifts out of narrative time – the recounting of narrative events relating to what is purportedly past experience – to refer to himself or the audience as participants in the present storytelling event; that is, they are the overtly and explicitly social interactional elements of his discourse.

A series of examples will illustrate the range of functions served by metanarrational statements in the two later versions of the story. Consider the following passage from the episode in which Bell discovers the giant tree in the 1979 telling:

> And I don't blame y'all if you don't believe me about this tree, because I wouldn't believe it either if I hadn'ta seen it with my own eyes. I don't know whether I can tell ya how you could believe it or not, but that was a big tree.

This passage is doubly metanarrational. First, it addresses and comments on the communicative interaction of the storytelling situation by commenting on Bell's own ability to induce the audience to believe his account and the problem of whether his hearers are moved to belief. On the face of it, what is at issue is the efficacy of the narrative communication. Below the surface, of course, is a second metamessage: The passage is also a comment on the believability of the story itself, a larger issue, to which we will return in a moment.

The second metanarrational passage in the same episode is explanatory, a stepping outside the narrative to clarify part of the action for those not fully familiar with the practices recounted:

> You know, we all put a X on a bee tree, for a brand. Which is a pretty good idea, to brand anything, you know, to kinda own it. It's ownership.

In the 1982 text, the first metanarrational statement in the discovery of the tree episode is directed at establishing a link between the audience's knowledge and experience and a feature of the narrative, an identificational device that elicits the participatory energies of the audience by matching their experience to Ed Bell's: "You've heard o' those big ol', uh, trees in California, you know, bein' so big." The second is self-referential, telling the audience more about Ed Bell the person, whose identity extends beyond the narrated event to encompass the present as well: "That's what I always think of, get some honey, you know, or get whatever's there to be gotten." As the preceding statement links the audience to the narrated event, this one links Ed Bell as narrator to Ed Bell as story protagonist across the time gap between narrated event and narrative event.

In addition to these various kinds of fully metanarrational statements, illustrated from the discovery of the tree episode, Bell resorts in his later tellings of the story to a series of more economical devices that index the storytelling interaction, more fleeting, but nevertheless effective, shifts of footing (Goffman 1981:124–57). These include brief references to himself as speaker and to the audience, appended to statements that are otherwise framed in narrative time. Examples would include, *"I tell you* I's astonished"* (1979), *"Folks,* we sure did have to run to get out of the way of that tree" (1979), "Well, *you know* I was really intrigued" (1982), "and *do you know* they's just a solid stream o' honey started runnin' out o' that thing?" (1982), or "That honey, *now folks,* was till pourin' out o' that six inch hole" (1982).

All of these, like the more extended metanarrational statements, have the effect of bridging the gap between the narrated event and the storytelling event by reaching out phatically to the audience, giving identificational and participatory immediacy to the story. This is especially useful at the beginning and the end of the narrative, to help effect the transition from the present situation to the narrated event in story time and then back again. Metanarrational elements of the kinds we have been discussing, both full statements and phatic gestures, tend to be especially notable in Ed Bell's later stories in the opening and closing sections of the narrative, the orientation and first episode and the coda, although he continues to employ them throughout the story to maintain the links between past and immediately current events.

Reference to the storytelling interaction is but one dimension of metanarration; equally important in these narratives is reference to the story itself. The tall tale is a genre of exaggeration, surprise, awe, in which the phenomenal world is stretched to – and beyond – the limits of one's prior experience and expectation. At the same time, however, the effect of the tall tale depends heavily on its apparent nature as a true personal experience narrative. The traditional tall tale, then, always makes some claims on our belief even as it exceeds plausibility (cf. Ben-Amos 1976:28). Insofar as believability is always at issue in the tall tale, any element that addresses believability is a metanarrational comment upon the story. Nor does this kind of metanarration need to involve a shift out of story time; action statements like, "I started up on a tree one day that I didn't believe. I couldn't believe my eyes," in the 1971 version of The Bee Tree, comment on the story at the same time that they carry forward the narrative action. In the later tellings, though, this metanarrational dimension of narrative action is greatly expanded, operating in conjunction with the frame shifting metanarration that indexes the storytelling event and is absent from the early version (cf. Tedlock 1972b).

As suggested earlier, the episode in the later versions in which Bell asks his father's permission to cut the bee tree serves *primarily* the metanarrational purpose of highlighting the issue of exaggeration and believability. This is accomplished through his father's expressions of doubt about the tree that Bell has described to him: "Buddy, you got the foolishest notions I ever heard of. . . . Your imagination just runs wild with you" (1979), and "Buddy, you got the strongest imagination of anybody I ever heard tell of . . . you know there's not any tree that big down there" (1982). Nor do his friends believe him; they laugh at what they take to be his joking about the fantastic tree, but go along with him, thinking he is just trying to arrange a picnic (1979).

The issue is raised yet again when Bell and his companions get out to the tree. In the 1979 version, he says, "Nobody else as far as I know had ever seen that tree in that whole country. 'Cause it was astonishingly big, everybody would've known about it if anybody's seen it." In the 1982 text, the same metanarrational business is accomplished by this passage:

> We got down there and those boys was . . . were enthralled. I'm tellin' you, they couldn't believe it. They said, "Ed, we've been here for years and we've never seen that tree. We still don't believe it's a bee tree."
> I said, "Well, I don't either. We're all even."

And still again, when Bell sees one of the branches of the tree expand and contract like bellows because of what will later prove to be a mass of squirrels inside it: "Just a crazy tree anyhow." The point is that by contrast with Bell's single statement of his own incredulous reaction to the tree in the 1971 version, the later versions detail the incredulity of others as well – his father and friends – stacking up expressions that keep the issue of believability before us as they expand the narrative.

Narrative change in relationship to context

In attempting to account for the greatly increased length and elaboration of Ed Bell's stories across the interval from the earliest recorded texts to the most recent ones, we have examined the proliferation of episodes, the insertion of new motifs and other elements of content, the increased use of direct discourse, the exploitation of repetitive devices such as syntactic and thematic parallelism, and the introduction of an important metanarrational dimension into the later tellings. That examination has been a step toward telling us in formal terms *what* the changes have been and opens the way for a consideration of *why* Bell has transformed his storytelling style in recent years. In particular, how can the changes we have seen in the stories be related to the changing contexts of his storytelling performance?

Ed Bell's early experience as a storyteller, as a young man, was shaped by his exposure to others who were traditional storytellers themselves, and occurred in traditional contexts such as the hunting campfires mentioned earlier. In these contexts, the participants were familiar with the traditional narrative genres of the culture, some of them storytellers themselves who competed for the opportunity to offer their stories to the group. Bell remembers this dynamic especially as a curb on prolixity:

> You know, when we used to tell these stories, we was out around a campfire, and uh, you know, you don't have long to tell a story. The other fella's just waitin' there, right now, he . . . he wants to tell *his* story. You got to make it just as short as you can, so you can cut off every limb that's in the way – just go right down the center.

That is, one of the narrative ground rules in the storytelling milieu in which Bell first participated as a young man held that one could not monopolize the floor too long; this proviso demanded at least a degree of economy in the telling of a story.

When first recorded by Pat Mullen, the fishing camp at Indianola was the scene of Ed Bell's storytelling performances. Here, his most appreciative audience, including his most regular customers, were fishermen, hunters, sportsmen, friends from the region. They too were familiar with the tall-tale genre and with the rural world reflected in the stories. But storytelling was clearly an activity of subordinate importance at the camp. For the most part, Bell was kept busy accommodating his customers, whose primary interest was to get out fishing. Thus, there were factors there too, as at the hunting campfires, that dictated a measure of economy in telling stories: "those people down there wouldn't stand around and listen very long. . . . They was wantin' to go fishin' or do something a lot o' the time." Only when the weather turned bad was there time for more extended storytelling, but then only until the weather improved or the customers gave up and went home.

The circumstances of the early years in Caldwell County and the long period on the Gulf coast contrast markedly with the period since 1976, during which Ed Bell has developed more and more into a public performer. His current audiences, for one thing, are very different from his earlier ones: city people attending urban folk festivals, young children in schools, members of civic clubs, university students. The members of his current audiences are far less knowledgeable about the agrarian world of farming, fishing, and hunting reflected in the tall tales than were his hunting friends and fishing camp customers. From his reading of his new audiences, Bell believes that they need to have more explained to them in order to make the tales accessible to them, making for more detail, like the explanation of branding the tree to establish a claim to it, or of the kind of tackle used to catch redfish (cf. Crowley 1966:111; Dégh 1969:228), as well as more redundancy, effected by repetitive constructions. Repetition, we should note, does not simply intensify a point by restating it, but ties the narration together in webs of cohesion that help an audience unfamiliar with traditional storytelling to hold together a story in their minds, the kind of effect that Boodberg (1954) identifies as the stereoscopic effect of parallelism and Hankiss as semantic oscillation (1981).

"Down on the coast," Bell told me, "everybody knew all this stuff, so I didn't have to describe it in detail. I go into more detail now, to be sure."

In addition to their lack of familiarity with rural life, the people who listen to Ed Bell's stories now are less knowledgeable about the conventions of traditional storytelling and the genre of the tall tale. Tall tales start out as apparently true narratives of personal experience, offered to be believed, with their ultimate effect traditionally derived by gradually bending the account out of shape – stretching the bounds of credibility bit by bit – until it finally reveals itself as a lie. Understatement and a low-key economy of presentation are stylistically and rhetorically useful in the traditional tall tale. But for an audience who know neither the genre nor the rural world on which it is based, the storyteller has an impulse both to embellish the element of exaggeration and to guide them along to an understanding of it. In response to my query, after telling "The Bee Tree" to my university class, Bell confessed, "Sometimes I think that a bunch of lovely youngsters like y'all'll stand a little bit more unrealistic stuff." Thus, Bell sacrifices the delicacy with which credibility was traditionally manipulated in the tall tale and telegraphs the lying aspect of the story through metanarration. This accounts in large part for the repeated metanarrational emphasis he places in his later tellings on belief and credibility. There is a generic transformation in process here, transforming the tall tale into a broader and more clearly exaggerated fiction than the classic traditional form (cf. Mullen 1978:148).

We may account for other dimensions of Bell's metanarration in terms of the changes in circumstances of his storytelling as well. Just as his current audiences are not familiar with either the tall tale or the experiential world in which it is grounded, they are not personally familiar with Bell himself or with his life history. His boyhood friends in Caldwell County knew him well, and his customers at the fishing camp knew him in the milieu that conditioned the content of his stories and his place within that milieu. To the people who hear him now, though, Bell is a stranger, about whom they know nothing but what they are told when he is introduced, which usually consists of a few details about his background and his achievements as a public storyteller. Accordingly, he has found it necessary over the past few years to attend more than formerly to the creation and management of a narrative persona in his stories (cf. Mullen 1978:146–7), telling things about himself that bear upon his involvement as protagonist in his stories. The result is more self-referencing metanarration, to fill in information that his former audiences already knew.

In addition to bridging the personal distance of the performance situation by revealing and offering himself to the audience through self-referencing discourse, Bell is at pains to elicit the interactive participation of his auditors by other means as well. Telling his stories in public performance contexts has tended to set him apart from his audience, with a marked distinction between performer and audience. These new contexts have a different participatory structure than the intimate, face-to-face contexts in which his earlier performances took place – the audience tends to be more passive, less inclined toward active participation. In response, Bell attempts to elicit their participatory involvement in the performance through the metanarrational channel, employing direct address and various forms of identificational metanarration: "It seems to me it makes them settle in better to listen to it. 'Well, folks, I'd like to tell you about this,' you know? 'Well, if he'd like to tell us,' why, they'd like to listen and they are part of the show then."

Still, it remains clear that Ed Bell is *the* performer in the event; there is not, as formerly, competition for the floor. Moreover, his current performances are organized first and foremost as storytelling events, not as incidental to fishing or some other activity. While it is true that an audience at a folk festival may be distracted away by some other activity on the festival grounds, some listeners always remain. Thus, Bell is relieved of the interactional pressure of a story exchange situation in which someone is waiting eagerly for a turn at narration. He is assured of his time on stage, featured as a virtuoso performer, and his performance is precisely what his audience is there for. This, in conjunction with the other factors we have considered, is strongly conducive to fuller, more elaborate performance. In his own words,

> When I get, ah, get out tellin' stories somewhere to a storytellin' crowd, why I like to make it a little longer because it keeps 'em from hearin' the end of it all at once, you know, keeps 'em in suspense a little bit longer, and that's really the reason that I put so much extra into 'em. It makes it a little bit better sometimes.

By contrast with his storytelling on the coast, "I don't have any trouble gettin' 'em to listen now. I can tell . . . add as much as I think is necessary."

But this does not mean that the stories are infinitely expandable; there are esthetic and performance limits of which he is quite consciously aware: "Sometimes you can draw one out a little too far and you begin to lose the interest of the people. But if you'll just keep on drawin' it out as far as you can and then spring the punch line on 'em pretty quick," the performance will be maximally effective. And again, "You've got to prepare the listener for a climax and everything you can put in that story to drag it out a little, make it more interesting, is fine, unless it . . . too much and it doesn't do any good then." Above all, Bell considers it crucially necessary to maintain a keen awareness of the audience as he performs:

> When I add it there I can look and watch people, how they receive it. You know, it doesn't take long when you're talkin' for someone to tell how they receive what you're sayin', and, uh, I can almost all the time tell if that was good, better, or worse.

I have emphasized in the foregoing discussion the transformative effect that Ed Bell's recent career as a public storyteller has had upon his tales, contrasting his earlier tellings, rooted in small-scale, face-to-face storytelling contexts with his far longer and more elaborate performances before public audiences. It is important to point out, however, that of the later texts presented in this paper, only two (the 1982 version of "The Bee Tree" and the text of "Redfishing in a Fog Bank" presented in the Appendix) were recorded before public audiences, whereas the remaining two were recorded in the intimate settings of Bell's home and my own, with only three or four others present. Yet the style is consistent throughout. More generally, I can state on the basis of an examination of texts of Bell's tall tales recorded over the past four years – in situations ranging from sessions involving only the two of us to large statewide folk festivals – that his style remains much the same, contrasting markedly with what is to be heard on Mullen's early recordings. How is it possible, then, to uphold the argument I have put forward concerning the formative influence of context on Bell's storytelling?

The answer lies in two related factors. First, context is more than simply a matter of situational setting, identified in objective terms. Far more important, as Goffman (1974) and others have told us repeatedly, is the participant's sense of "what it is that is going on here." And for Ed Bell now, the preeminent factor is his definition of a situation in which he tells stories in his own current identity as a public storyteller, a recognized public performer. His old storytelling venues, around the campfire or at the fishing camp, no longer figure in his current life; when he tells stories now, he tells them in the manner appropriate to the settings that sustain his identity as a storyteller, and those are all public occasions in which he is set off as a performer from his audience.

In addition, the act of recording itself now contributes to and upholds the sense that even one-to-one sessions with a fieldworker implicate larger audiences of strangers: The tapes are to be heard by others, perhaps played to classes, or broadcast, or printed in a book. That makes any recording a public performance, no matter how intimate the recording session and even in the physical absence of the audience. That is why a tall tale told with only myself and the tape recorder present will begin, "Well, folks. . . ." The differences between Ed Bell's current stories and his earlier ones are rooted in the shifting contexts of his storytelling, but there is a halo effect at work here – he is a public storyteller now, whether or not the public is present.

Among the many significant discoveries made by Albert Lord in his influential studies of the oral poetic process was that the South Slavic *guslars* whom he and Milman Parry recorded tended to produce their longest, most elaborate texts under the special conditions of dictating them to the fieldworker (Lord 1953). Lord concludes that the usual conditions of epic song performance, in which the singer had to adapt his performance to an audience at a coffeehouse or celebration, for example, imposed limits on the productions of the best performers, making their songs shorter and less elaborate than they were *capable* of achieving. Dictation for the receptive fieldworker in situations organized solely as occasions for the singers to display their art removed those constraints; it enabled the great Avdo Mededović, for example, to compose songs approximating the length of the *Odyssey*. Indeed, Lord goes on to suggest on the basis of this discovery that the Homeric poems themselves are "oral dictated texts," produced to be recorded rather than in more conventional performance contexts. The point is that when the epic singers were freed from the usual contextual factors that constrained their performance, and placed in contexts whose very purpose was to allow them to display their talents, they took advantage of the situation to exercise their full virtuosity in the production of long, elaborate texts.

Much the same, I would argue, appears to have happened in Ed Bell's storytelling. Freed from the contextual pressures that favored relative brevity in storytelling at the hunting campfire or fishing camp, such as competition for the floor or the lure of fishing, and singled out to perform at festivals and other public events because of folklorists' recognition of his great talent as a storyteller, Bell has cultivated that virtuosity. At the same time, he has become more distanced from his audience, both interactionally and by culture and background, in the performance situations themselves. Under these new conditions, feeling both the opportunity to display his storytelling art to the fullest and the desire to bridge the personal and experiential gap between himself and his auditors, Bell has made his stories longer and more elaborate. Even more, his view of himself has been transformed from someone who "never used to think of myself as a storyteller" to someone who is preeminently a storyteller, always responsible for the full display of his competence whether a full audience is present or not.

Certain implications in this process warrant the attention of those engaged in staging folklife festivals and other programs for the public presentation of folk artists. Such programs may well provide folk artists with opportunities for a fuller exercise of their artistic virtuosity than they might enjoy in local, more traditional settings, but their art and their lives may also be irreversibly transformed in the process. The assumption that public display of authentic folk tradition fosters its maintenance and preservation is ideologically appealing, but dangerously simplistic. If we are to persist in intervening in folk tradition, we need to look far more closely and carefully at the effects of our efforts on the artists and traditions on whose behalf we claim to be working.

Appendix

Redfishing in a Fog Bank (1982)
When I was stayin' over there by Houston for a few nights, we lived about a hundred 'n' thirty-nine miles from Houston, when we were

on the coast, but I was stayin' over close to Houston. I don't remember what for. And one o' those Houston boys says, "Hey, Ed, let's go redfishin' tomorrow."

I said, "Where?"

He said, "Oh, prob'ly down 'bout Offut's Bayou, towards Galveston."

I said, "Well, I don't know nothin' about it, you gonna have to point the way."

"Oh, we're not goin' till mornin'. There's that fog gets rough at night, and we couldn't stay out there all night in that fog – we'd be drippin' wet."

So, "O.K."

He says, "I'll be over early in the mornin' to pick you up, now."

"O.K."

Next morning, he's out there, blowin' 'is horn, people 'round there hollerin', sayin' "Shut that noise up!" and all that kind o' stuff. I had to get in the car with 'im and take off in a hurry, keep 'em from gettin' after us rougher.

And I says, "What in the world you blowin' the horn here for, feller?"

He said, "Man, it's almost fishin' time and the fog's so bad I can't drive fast." Said, "We got to go on down there right just quick as we can." Says, "Early fishin's all that's any good."

So he's takin' off down the road to Galveston, and he's lookin' over the side o' the car, with his head hangin' out the door watchin' that white stripe. That's the only way he could see the pavement at all. And I couldn't see it myself – I didn't know what he's doin', just bumpin' along the road.

And he drove and he drove and he drove; finally, he said, "Well . . . ," pulled out . . . seemed like he pulled over a little bit. Says, "Here we are. Get out and let's fish."

Well folks, that sounds idiotic. You know, you can't see anything, you can't hear nothin', and you're at the water. I didn't hardly believe it, but I'd . . . O.K.

I wasn't in no hurry gettin' out. He done got out and baited his hooks. We used, uh, two hooks about this far apart [holds hands about eight inches apart] on a double-drop leader to tight line for redfish, with a four-ounce pyramid lead sinker on there, great big ol' heavy pole, and you'd rear back like that and let that thing go through there and it'll travel too, it'll go a long ways.

So he got out there and cast it out and I was listenin' and listenin'. Huh! I can hear a four-ounce sinker splash for 400 yards. I ain't heard no splash. I say, what if he's roped a brahma bull? I got back over by the car door. I's gonna get back inside if he'd roped a brahma bull, cause some o' those brahmas get bad.

And about that time, why, I noticed his pole doing that way [jiggling forefinger]. I said, "That's just exactly like he had a redfish." And he brought that thing on in, and he had an eight-pound redfish.

Folks, I'm tellin' you, I . . . I . . . I was . . . I was really certified in a hurry. I knew he was right. So I grabbed my pole out and he says, "Come on, Ed, fishin'."

Well, you know, I was tryin' to do too fast, and I couldn't bait my hook, I stuck the hook in my fingers, and all that. Finally, I got ready, I reared back and let that thing go, still feelin' silly folks, just know I'm gon' catch that brahma bull. I don't see no water, they ain't no water down there. I didn't hear no splash.

There it is! There it is! I'm sittin' there fightin' one o' them big ol' eight-pound redfish, and I'm fightin' him hard.

Well, I fought and fought him and brought him on in. Golly, that's a nice fish.

Folks, we got sixteen o' those big reds, and the fog lifted, and we's fifteen miles from the bay. We'd been fishin' in a fog bank.

(Recorded at the University of Texas, November 11, 1982)[2]

The Wonderful Hunt

You know, folks, we lived on a river. At least it was only about a mile down t' the river, and I decided I wanted'a go huntin', kill some geese. So I went and asked papa if I could use his muzzle-loader, go down there to the island, kill a bunch o' geese, middle o' that river.

He said, "Son, I haven't seen a goose on that river in five or six years."

I said, "Papa, I got lots o' patience."

Well, the old man taught me patience, he taught me how to track, trail, and everything like that, how to shoot guns, all kinds o' guns.

So, I said, "Papa, I'd like to take your old double-barreled muzzle-loader down there and get some geese."

He said, "Well, son, I like to see you get to huntin' and learn things," and he said, "you don't need . . . there's nothin' to do now anyway, it's winter time, so you might as well go down there and hunt a while. You better get your mama to fix you some sandwiches."

So mama heard us talkin', she's already fixin' the sandwiches

---

² Motif X1156 Lie: other unusual methods of catching fish; X1651.3.1 Fish swim in fog Baughman 1966; Thompson 1955–8).

outa cornbread, you know, how you cut that cornbread up in sections out of a pan, sliced open, and she put some meat, like that good stuff we had for supper, you know, she put that in there, or some sausage, or somethin'. I put a bunch o' them up, took 'em down there t'the river, had my hip boots on, and I had this ol' muzzle-loader with me.

And papa had a . . . had one o' those, uh . . . tampin' rods that they used to pack a charge in there, you know, and he told me, said, "Now son, don't you lose that rod." Said, "If you lose that rod it'd break my heart. You see on the end o' that rod, look there, there's two rows, and those are diamonds, those are not even pearls, they're diamonds." And they just fit an ordinary person's hand – one row'd be down below, and one row up there. Then a little knob and a . . . looked like an ice-pick run on up about fourteen inches, well, everything like that, and that was the prettiest ramrod I'd ever seen. Papa said, "You lose that, son, they ain't much use you comin' back home." Well, the old man was strict, now, I'll tell you that old man was strict.

Well I went on down t'the river, hip boots and all. I got down to the river, why I started wadin' across and it was a little deeper water than I thought. I'd waded across there several times with hip boots and hadn't got any water in my boots. This time I had to tiptoe. Then I got just a little bit o' water in there, but what . . . what mind? Little water ain't gonna hurt me.

I sat down there out on that island, I sat there all day. I ain't seen or heard of geese. I sat there for five days and nights, and I ain't seen nor heard of a thing. And on the day o' the next day, why, I was settin' there and I was beginnin' to look pretty steadily, look up thisaway and that way, then I'd give this charge with the ramrod another good seatin' down, you know, 'cause every time you pack it it'd shoot a little harder. I got it all fixed up pretty good.

And I was settin' there on this island and all at once I heard a "nyaw, nyaw, nyaw, nyaw." I looked up and there came a thousand geese swimmin' down that river. A whole thousand of 'em! I wanna tell you, it had me goin'. I said, "What in the world . . . that's a nice bunch o' geese!

'Bout that time, I heard a "quack, quack, quack; quack-qu-quack quack quack, quack, quack." I looked down the river, and there came a thousand ducks, swimmin' up it. You know, that's gettin' somethin' nice, now, I'm gettin' this stuff together. It was worth waitin' for.

And you know, lookin' back and forth thisaway, why, I looked across the river to where I'd waded in, there stood a deer had seventy-five points. Man, that was the most magnificent buck I'd ever seen in all my life.

[*R.B.:* You don't see those seventy-five pointers very often.]

Not often, that's the reason I was so excited. And all at once I heard somethin' go "arrr, rrrr, rowf!" Looked over my shoulder and there was a grizzly bear. And he got mad at me movin' my shoulders around, he didn't like me a bit.

Aw, huh! Doggone, I . . . I . . . I don't know what to do, and about that time I heard a "bzzzzzzrrrrr." And I looked down between my legs; you know, I'd been settin' there six days, and those nights gettin' cold, and that big ol' rattlesnake, big ol' diamondback, crawled up there and coiled up between my legs. Well, I just knew I was a goner. Ain't no way to live over it. Ain't no way.

And I looked over there at that deer, and I said, "By golly, I ain't never in my life killed a decent buck. I'm gon' kill me a good deer. To heck with everything else!"

And I got so worried 'bout all this stuff, didn't know half what I's doin'. I just leveled down across the river, and I pulled both barrels [mimes pulling of trigger].

That ol' gun blew up – I'd been tampin' those charges too heavy, there was somethin' else the matter too. That gun blew up, one barrel went up the river and killed those thousand geese. The other barrel went down the river and killed those thousand ducks. Stock flew over m'shoulder and knocked the grizzly bear in the head. Killed 'im. Trigger guard went down and cut the snake's head off, killed him.

Well, I jumped out there in that water and started grabbin' up these geese and these ducks. You know it's a hard job to gather up a thousand geese and a thousand ducks. But I was gatherin' all them up just fast as I could.

And as I was goin' out around close to where that buck was, I looked at him. I says, "Wait a minute. One barrel had to go up the river and kill those thousand geese. The other barrel went down the river and killed those thousand ducks. What killed that deer?" I got over there and looked at him real close and there's a big ol' hole 'bout that big around [makes circle of thumb and forefinger] right through him. He's dead.

Then I saw right on the other side, big ol' tree, just split open, layin' out like that [moves touching palms apart]. I says, "Oh, my goodness, that ramrod! Papa's gonna kill me sure as the world outa that ramrod." I'd forgot it in that gun. That was partly what blowed it up.

Well, I don't know what to do. I just don't know anything t'do.

Whichever way I go, it looks like I'm gon' get killed, or somethin'.

So I went back and gathered up . . . no, I didn't gather . . . gathered up the rest o' those ducks. Every time I'd walk outa the water, there I'd dump these boots, the fish outa my boots, 'cause they was full of 'em – those big hip boots full o' fish. Well, I got a great big ol' pile o' fish out there, and I got these thousand geese and a thousand ducks. I went back to look at that deer again, and I was nearly cryin' by that time. And I looked at that big ol' tree over there all split open, layin' out like that. I looked, and there was another'n same way. I says, "Wait a minute. I believe there's that ramrod down there." So I took off down that way, and in a minute about a hundred yards in front of me, why there was that ramrod, it had . . . it was stickin' in the side of a great big ol' tree an' it had nine quail pinned on it.

(Recorded at Bauman's home, Austin, November 11, 1982)[3]

---

[3] Type 1980 The Lucky Shot, and subdivisions 1890B Bursting Gun and Series of Lucky Accidents and 1890D Ramrod Shot; 1894 Man Shoots a Ramrod Full of Ducks; 1895 A Man Wading in Water Catches Many Fish in his Boots. Motifs X1110 Wonderful hunt; X1111 Hunter shoots ramrod full of ducks; X1112 Hunter catches fish in boots while wading; X1124 Lie: the hunter catches or kills game by ingenious or unorthodox method; X1234(a) Large deer; X1258 Lies about geese (Baughman 1966; Thompson 1955–8). For another published version of "The Wonderful Hunt" as told by Ed Bell, see Sitton (1983:168–70).

6
CONCLUSION

Story, performance, and event: These are the cornerstones on which I have endeavored to construct a framework tying together narrated events, narrative texts, and narrative events, as part of a larger concern with the constitutive role of discourse in social life. As I have noted in the Introduction, however, the double grounding of narrative in human events that has concerned me here is no new discovery. It is certainly not my discovery; I have cited Walter Benjamin's felicitously economical statement of the interrelationship and have adopted Roman Jakobson's terms, "narrated event" and "narrative event" for the twin social anchor points of narrative discourse. And, to carry my argument still further, I offer still another formulation of the crucial nexus that occupies us here, this one by Mikhail Bakhtin:

> before us are two events – the event that is narrated in the work and the event of narration itself (we ourselves participate in the latter, as listeners or readers); these events take place in different times (which are marked by different durations as well) and in different places, but at the same time these two events are indissolubly united in a single but complex event that we might call the work in the totality of all its events, including the external material givenness of the work, and its text, and the world represented in the text, and the author-creator and the listener or reader; thus we perceive the fullness of the work in all its wholeness and indivisibility, but at the same time we understand the diversity of the elements that constitute it. (Bakhtin 1981:255)

I make a special point of this long-standing recognition of the double grounding of narrative in events only partly as a warrant for my own investigations. My other reason for this marshaling of authority is to cast into relief just how little the insights of Benjamin, Jakobson, Bakhtin, and others have been pursued in the integrative terms they would seem inescapably to suggest. For the truth is that the indivisible work of which Bakhtin writes has indeed been divided in conventional scholarly practice. But now that I have attempted to demonstrate by example how it might be put back together, I want to capitalize on such persuasive power as the results may have to argue that we have, in fact, reached a point beyond which further disciplinary parochialism would defeat the very purposes that at least some students of narrative are beginning to profess from their respective disciplinary vantage points.

Recent critical theory, for example, with the waning of structuralism, has begun to mount a double attack on the autonomous narrative text, recontextualizing it from the vantage points of both author and reader. In reader-response criticism, in all its various guises, the focus is on the role of the reader, no longer as a passive receiver of the meaning inherent in the text, but as an active participant in the actualization – indeed, the production – of textual meaning as an interpretive accomplishment, much like the members of an oral storytelling audience (see, e.g., Tompkins 1980). One also finds in reader-response criticism and other lines of analysis convergent with it (e.g., Chambers 1984; Hutcheon 1984) a concern with the formal devices employed by the author to engage the participatory involvement of the reader, again as an oral storyteller would do, such as metanarration, the textual creation of a communicative context for the narration, the leaving of gaps to be filled by the reader, and so on. This effort to resituate the literary narrative text in a web of communicative relationships and processes has, not surprisingly, induced some literary theorists to begin to consider – but only in a programmatic way as yet – that it might be productive to think of literary narration as akin to oral storytelling (Fowler 1981; Pratt 1977; Smith 1981).

In anthropology, too, there are signs of a new interest in storytelling, stimulated by an emergent reorientation in the discipline more generally, away from conceptions of society and culture as abstract, normative, collective structures and toward an understanding of social and cultural life as forms of symbolic production, the situated social accomplishments of people engaged in the practice of social life. When one looks to the social practices by which social life is accomplished, one finds – with surprising frequency – people telling stories to each other, as a means of giving cognitive and emotional coherence to experience, constructing and negotiating social identity (Herzfeld 1985:206–31; Myerhoff 1978); investing the experiential landscape with moral significance in a way that can be brought to bear on human behavior (Keith Basso 1984); generating, interpreting, and transforming the work experience (Schwartzman 1984); and a host of other reasons. Narrative here is not merely the reflection of culture, or the external charter of social institutions, or the cognitive arena for sorting out the logic of cultural codes, but is constitutive of social life in the act of storytelling. There is not much here – at least not yet – of literariness, or of performance as a special mode of communication, but there is a deep sense of context and of social action that is essential to any conception of literature as social practice.

Among linguists, an interest in storytelling has emerged chiefly among those concerned with conversational analysis, influenced as well by convergent approaches in linguistic anthropology and sociology addressing the use of language in the conduct of social life (see, e.g., Chafe 1980b; Sacks 1974; Tannen 1982, 1984). Again, as one approaches conversation, one encounters people telling stories; conversational analysis has made strong contributions to the discovery and elucidation of the structure of oral narratives as conversationally accomplished, to the acquisition of storytelling competence by children, and to form–function interrelationships in the recounting of stories in conversational encounters. The poetics of oral narrative, however, have not figured in such analysis (but cf. Polanyi 1982), and the relationship between narrative discourse and narrative events has yet to be explored in any systematic way.

In light of all these concurrent and potentially complementary inquiries into the form, function, and conduct of oral narration, the need appears all the compelling for a fusion of the various separate lines of investigation that have engaged the interest of the respective disciplines and that I have drawn together in the studies that make up this book. In a word, we need it all: a formal poetics of performance, an ethnographic understanding of events and social interaction in terms of the constitutive role of discourse, and a sense of form–function interrelationships.

I should make it clear that I am not advocating that we should move ahead to some sort of mechanically "interdisciplinary" effort that simply combines concepts and methods and analytical foci from a range of separate disciplines, for that is not what I have undertaken here. I resist this notion of interdisciplinary analysis on two grounds. First of all, to seek an "interdisciplinary" solution is to concede the legitimacy of disciplinary differentiation to begin with, whereas I have preferred to align myself with the integrative vision of language, literature, and culture in which folklore was itself first conceived. More particularly, though, with regard to narrative, I believe that "the fullness of the work in all its wholeness and indivisibility" demands and is better served by the kind of integrative vision offered by the performance-centered analysis I have pursued in these pages.

My analyses have focused principally on reported speech, the dynamics of expressive lying and fabrication, the forms and functions of metanarration, and the poetics of performance, all as keys to elucidating the devices and processes by which narrated events, narrative texts, and narrative events are inextricably linked. This hardly exhausts the possibilities, to be sure, but I would like to hope that I have demonstrated not only the productiveness of my unified perspective for the understanding of oral narrative "in the totality of all its events," but also how this integrative vision illuminates other more general concerns, such as stability and variation in the folkloric text, the problem of genre, and the rhetorical efficacy of literary forms. The multiple payoffs offered by such investigations are, I hope, evident, for in exploring the social nexus of oral storytelling we explore one of the most fundamental and potent foundations of our existence as social beings. And that reminds me of a story:[1]

---

[1]   I have lifted this joke from an essay by Alan Dundes (1977) but have made slight changes in the format.

A supercomputer is built and all the world's knowledge is pro-
grammed into it. A gathering of top scientists punch in the question:
"Will the computer ever replace man?"

Clickity, click, whir, whir, and the computer lights flash on and
off.

Finally a small printout emerges saying, "That reminds me of a
story."

REFERENCES

Abrahams, Roger D.
1977 Toward an Enactment-Centered Theory of Folklore. In *Frontiers of Folklore*, ed. William Bascom, pp. 79–120. Boulder: Westview Press for the AAAS.
1982 Storytelling Events: Wake Amusements and the Structure of Nonsense on St. Vincent. *Journal of American Folklore* 95:389–414.

Babcock, Barbara
1977 The Story in the Story: Metanarration in Folk Narrative. In *Verbal Art as Performance*, ed. Richard Bauman, repr. ed. 1984, pp. 61–79. Prospect Heights, Il: Waveland Press.

Bakhtin, Mikhail M.
1968 *Rabelais and His World*, transl. Hélène Iswolsky. Cambridge, MA: MIT Press.
1981 *The Dialogic Imagination*, transl. Caryl Emerson and Michael Holquist. Austin: University of Texas Press.

Bascom, William
1955 Verbal Art. *Journal of American Folklore* 68:245–52.
1965 The Forms of Folklore: Prose Narratives. *Journal of American Folklore* 78:3–20.

Basso, Ellen B.
1985 *A Musical View of the Universe*. Philadelphia: University of Pennsylvania Press.

Basso, Keith H.
1984 "Stalking with Stories": Names, Places, and Moral Narratives among the Western Apache. In *Text, Play, and Story: The Construction and Reconstruction of Self and Society*, ed. Edward M. Bruner, pp. 19–55. Washington DC: American Ethnological Society.

Baughman, Ernest W.
1966 *Type and Motif-Index of the Folktales of England and North America*. The Hague: Mouton.

Bauman, Richard
1972a The LaHave Island General Store: Sociability and Verbal Art in a Nova Scotia Community. *Journal of American Folklore* 85:330–43.
1972b Differential Identity and the Social Base of Folklore. In *Toward New Perspectives in Folklore*, ed. Américo Paredes and Richard Bauman, pp. 31–41. Austin: University of Texas Press.
1977a Linguistics, Anthropology, and Verbal Art: Toward a Unified Perspective, with a Special Discussion of Children's Folklore. In *Linguistics and Anthropology*, ed. Muriel Saville-Troike, pp. 13–36. Georgetown Uni-

117

versity Round Table on Languages and Linguistics 1977. Washington DC: Georgetown University Press.

1977b *Verbal Art as Performance,* repr. ed. 1984. Prospect Heights Il: Waveland Press.

1977c Settlement Patterns on the Frontiers of Folklore. In *Frontiers of Folklore,* ed. William Bascom, pp. 121–31. Boulder: Westview Press for the AAAS.

1981 "Any Man Who Keeps More'n One Hound'll Lie to You": Dog Trading and Storytelling at Canon, Texas. In *"And Other Neighborly Names": Social Process and Cultural Image in Texas Folklore,* ed. Richard Bauman and Roger D. Abrahams, pp. 79–103. Austin: University of Texas Press.

1982 Conceptions of Folklore in the Development of Literary Semiotics. *Semiotica* 39:1–20.

1983 The Field Study of Folklore in Context. In *Handbook of American Folklore,* ed. Richard M. Dorson, pp. 362–8. Bloomington: Indiana University Press.

1984 The Making and Breaking of Context in West Texas Oral Anecdotes. In *Meaning, Form, and Use in Context: Linguistic Applications,* ed. Deborah Schiffrin, pp. 160–74. Georgetown University Round Table on Languages and Linguistics 1984. Washington DC: Georgetown University Press.

Ben-Amos, Dan

1972 Toward a Definition of Folklore in Context. In *Toward New Perspectives in Folklore,* ed. Américo Paredes and Richard Bauman, pp. 3–15. Austin: University of Texas Press.

1975 *Sweet Words: Storytelling Events in Benin.* Philadelphia: ISHI.

1976 Talmudic Tall Tales. In *Folklore Today,* ed. Linda Dégh, Henry Glassie, and Felix J. Oinas, pp. 25–43. Bloomington: Indiana University.

1977 The Context of Folklore: Implications and Prospects. In *Frontiers of Folklore,* ed. William Bascom, pp. 36–53. Boulder: Westview Press for the AAAS.

Ben-Amos, Dan, and Kenneth S. Goldstein, eds.

1975 *Folklore: Performance and Communication.* The Hague: Mouton.

Benjamin, Walter

1969 *Illuminations.* New York: Schocken.

Berry, Jack

1961 *Spoken Art in West Africa.* London: School of Oriental and African Studies, University of London.

Bethke, Robert D.

1976 Storytelling at an Adirondack Inn. *Western Folklore* 35:123–39.

Biebuyck-Goetz, Brunhilde

1977 "This is the Dyin' Truth": Mechanisms of Lying. *Journal of the Folklore Institute* 14:73–95.

Bloch, Maurice

1975 *Political Oratory in Traditional Society.* New York: Academic.

Boatright, Mody C.
   1973[1961] The Oil Promoter as Trickster. In *Mody Boatright, Folklorist,* ed.
      Ernest Speck, pp. 145–62. Austin: University of Texas Press.
Bødker, Laurits
   1965 Anecdote. In *International Dictionary of Regional European Ethnology and
      Folklore,* vol. II, pp. 26–7. Copenhagen: Rosenkilde and Bagger.
Boodberg, P.A.
   1954 Syntactical metaplasia in stereoscopic parallelism. Cedules from a Berkeley
      Workshop in Asiatic Philology.
Booth, Wayne
   1983 *The Rhetoric of Fiction,* 2nd ed. Chicago: University of Chicago Press.
Botkin, Benjamin
   1949 Anecdote. In *Standard Dictionary of Folklore, Mythology, and Legend,* ed.
      Maria Leach, vol. 1, p. 56. New York: Funk and Wagnalls.
Bouissac, Paul
   1976 *Circus and Culture.* Bloomington: Indiana University Press.
Brandes, Stanley
   1980 *Metaphors of Masculinity: Sex and Status in Andalusian Folklore.* Phila-
      delphia: University of Pennsylvania Press.
Brenneis, Don
   1978 The Matter of Talk: Political Performances in Bhatgaon. *Language in So-
      ciety* 7:159–70.
Briggs, Charles L.
   1985 Treasure Tales and Pedagogical Discourse in *Mexicano* New Mexico. *Jour-
      nal of American Folklore* 98:287–314.
Brown, Penelope, and Stephen Levinson
   1978 Universals in Language Usage: Politeness Phenomena. In *Questions and
      Politeness,* ed. Esther N. Goody, pp. 56–289. Cambridge: Cambridge
      University Press.
Brunvand, Jan
   1961 An Indiana Storyteller Revisited. *Midwest Folklore* 11:5–14.
   1978 *The Study of American Folklore,* 2nd ed. New York: Norton.
Burke, Kenneth
   1937 *Attitudes Toward History,* vol. 1. New York: The New Republic.
   1941 Literature as Equipment for Living. In *The Philosophy of Literary Form,*
      pp. 293–304. Baton Rouge: Louisiana State University Press.
   1969[1950] *A Rhetoric of Motives.* Berkeley and Los Angeles: University of Cal-
      ifornia Press.
Burns, Allan F.
   1983 *An Epoch of Miracles: Oral Literature of the Yucatec Maya.* Austin: Uni-
      versity of Texas Press.
Carey, George
   1976 The Storyteller's Art and the Collector's Intrusion. In *Folklore Today,* ed.
      Linda Dégh, Henry Glassie, Felix J. Oinas, pp. 81–91. Bloomington:
      Indiana University.
Carson, Jane
   1965 *Colonial Virginians at Play.* Williamsburg, VA: Colonial Williamsburg.

Chafe, Wallace L.

1980a The Deployment of Consciousness in the Production of Narrative. In *The Pear Stories*, ed. Wallace L. Chafe, pp. 9–50. Norwood, NJ: Ablex.

1980b *The Pear Stories*. Norwood, NJ: Ablex.

Chambers, Ross

1984 *Story and Situation: Narrative Seduction and the Power of Fiction*. Minneapolis: University of Minnesota Press.

Chatman, Seymour

1978 *Story and Discourse: Narrative Structure in Fiction and Film*. Ithaca: Cornell University Press.

Coffin, Tristram P.

1968 *Our Living Traditions*. New York: Basic Books.

Colby, Benjamin N.

1973 A Partial Grammar of Eskimo Folktales. *American Anthropologist* 75:645–62.

Cosentino, Donald

1982 *Defiant Maids and Stubborn Farmers: Tradition and Invention in Mende Story Performance*. Cambridge: Cambridge University Press.

Cothran, Kay L.

1974 Talking Trash on the Okefenokee Swamp Rim, Georgia. *Journal of American Folklore* 87:340–56.

Craven, Wesley Frank

1949 *The Southern Colonies in the Seventeenth Century, 1607–1689*. Baton Rouge: Louisiana State University Press.

Crowley, Daniel J.

1966 *I Could Talk Old-Story Good: Creativity in Bahamian Folklore*. Berkeley and Los Angeles: University of California Press.

Culler, Jonathan

1981 *The Pursuit of Signs*. Ithaca: Cornell University Press.

Darnell, Regna

1974 Correlates of Cree Narrative Performance. In *Explorations in the Ethnography of Speaking*, ed. Richard Bauman and Joel Sherzer, pp. 315–36. Cambridge: Cambridge University Press.

Dégh, Linda

1969 *Folktales and Society*. Bloomington: Indiana University Press.

Dégh, Linda, and Andrew Vázsonyi

1976 Legend and Belief. In *Folklore Genres*, ed. Dan Ben-Amos, pp. 93–123. Austin: University of Texas Press.

Doložel, Lubomír

1980 Truth and Authenticity in Narrative. *Poetics Today* 1(3):7–25.

Dorson, Richard M.

1959 *American Folklore*. Chicago: University of Chicago Press.

1964 *Buying the Wind*. Chicago: University of Chicago Press.

Douglas, Mary

1968 The Social Control of Cognition: Some Factors in Joke Perception. *Man* 3:361–76.

Dundes, Alan
1964 *The Morphology of North American Indian Folktales*. Folklore Fellows Communication No. 195. Helsinki: Academia Scientiarum Fennica.
1977 Who Are the Folk? In *Frontiers of Folklore*, ed. William R. Bascom, pp. 17–35. Boulder: Westview Press for the AAAS.

Duranti, Alessandro
1980 *Láuga and Talanoaga: Structure and Variation in the Language of a Samoan Speech Event*. Working Papers in Sociolinguistics No. 72. Austin: Southwest Educational Development Laboratory.

Enkvist, Nils Erik
1981 Experiential Iconism in Text Strategy. *Text* 1:77–111.

Esar, Evan
1952 *The Humor of Humor*. New York: Bramhall House.

Falassi, Alessandro
1980 *Folklore by the Fireside: Text and Context of the Tuscan Veglia*. Austin: University of Texas Press.

Ferris, Bill
1977 *Ray Lum: Mule Trader, an Essay*. Memphis: Center for Southern Folklore.

Fine, Elizabeth C.
1984 *The Folklore Text: From Performance to Print*. Bloomington: Indiana University Press.

Finnegan, Ruth
1967 *Limba Stories and Storytelling*. Oxford: Clarendon Press.
1977 *Oral Poetry: Its Nature, Significance, and Social Context*. Cambridge: Cambridge University Press.

Firth, Raymond
1961 *Elements of Social Organization*. 3rd ed. Boston: Beacon Press.

Fiske, John
1904 *Civil Government in the United States*. Boston: Houghton-Mifflin.

Fowler, Roger
1981 *Literature as Social Discourse*. Bloomington: Indiana University Press.

Fox, James J.
1977 Roman Jakobson and the Comparative Study of Parallelism. In *Roman Jakobson: Echoes of His Scholarship*, ed. J.D. Armstrong and C.H. van Schooneveld, pp. 59–90. Lisse: Peter de Ridder.

Galin, Anne
1981 Semantics and Structure: An Analysis of Two Trickster Tales. *Text* 1:241–68.

Genette, Gérard
1980 *Narrative Discourse*. Ithaca: Cornell University Press.

Georges, Robert
1969 Toward an Understanding of Story-Telling Events. *Journal of American Folklore* 82:313–29.
1971 The General Concept of Legend: Some Assumptions to Be Reexamined and Reassessed. In *American Folk Legend: A Symposium*, ed. Wayland D. Hand, pp. 1–19. Berkeley and Los Angeles: University of California Press.

Gilsenan, Michael

1976 Lying, Honor, and Contradiction. In *Transaction and Meaning: Directions in the Anthropology of Exchange and Symbolic Behavior,* ed. Bruce Kapferer, pp. 191–219. Philadelphia: Institute for the Study of Human Issues.

Goffman, Erving

1959 *The Presentation of Self in Everyday Life.* New York: Doubleday Anchor.

1967 Where the Action Is. In *Interaction Ritual.* New York: Doubleday Anchor.

1971 *Relations in Public.* New York: Basic Books.

1974 *Frame Analysis.* New York: Harper & Row.

1981 *Forms of Talk.* Philadelphia: University of Pennsylvania Press.

Goody, Jack

1977 *The Domestication of the Savage Mind.* Cambridge: Cambridge University Press.

Green, Ben K.

1968 *Horse Tradin'.* New York: Knopf.

1972 *Some More Horse Tradin'.* New York: Knopf.

Halliday, M.A.K. and Ruqaiya Hasan

1976 *Cohesion in English.* London: Longmans.

Halpert, Herbert

1971 Definition and Variation in Folk Legend. In *American Folk Legend: A Symposium,* ed. Wayland D. Hand, pp. 47–54. Berkeley and Los Angeles: University of California Press.

Hankiss, Elemér

1981 Semantic Oscillation: A Universal of Artistic Expression. In *The Sign in Music and Literature,* ed. Wendy Steiner, pp. 67–85. Austin: University of Texas Press.

Heath, Shirley Brice

1983 *Ways with Words.* Cambridge: Cambridge University Press.

Herskovits, Melville J.

1961 The Study of African Oral Art. *Journal of American Folklore* 74:451–6.

Herzfeld, Michael

1985 *The Poetics of Manhood: Contest and Identity in a Cretan Mountain Village.* Princeton: Princeton University Press.

Hutcheon, Linda

1984 *Narcissistic Narrative: The Metafictional Paradox.* New York: Methuen.

Hymes, Dell

1974 Ways of Speaking. In *Explorations in the Ethnography of Speaking,* ed. Richard Bauman and Joel Sherzer, pp. 433–51. Cambridge: Cambridge University Press.

1975 Folklore's Nature and the Sun's Myth. *Journal of American Folklore* 88:345–69.

1981 *"In Vain I Tried to Tell You": Essays in Native American Ethnopoetics.* Philadelphia: University of Pennsylvania Press.

1985 Language, Memory, and Selective Performance: Cultee's "Salmon's Myth" as Twice Told to Boas. 98:391–434.

Jakobson, Roman

1966 Grammatical Parallelism and its Russian Facet. *Language* 42:398–429.

1968 Poetry of Grammar and Grammar of Poetry. *Lingua* 21:597–609.

1971[1957] Shifters, Verbal Categories, and the Russian Verb. In *Roman Jakobson: Selected Writings, vol. 2,* pp. 130–47. The Hague: Mouton.

Jakobson, Roman, and Krystyna Pomorska

1983 *Dialogues.* Cambridge, MA: MIT Press.

Jason, Heda

1971 The Narrative Structure of Swindler Tales. *Arv* 27:141–60.

Jasper, Patricia

1979 *Ed Bell, Storyteller.* Videotape, color, 30 min. Austin: Austin Community Television.

Labov, William

1972 The Transformation of Experience in Narrative Syntax. In *Language in the Inner City,* pp. 354–96. Philadelphia: University of Pennsylvania Press.

1979 *A Grammar of Narrative.* Lecture presented at the University of Texas at Austin, October 10, 1979.

1982 Speech Actions and Reactions in Personal Narrative. In *Analyzing Discourse: Text and Talk,* ed. Deborah Tannen, pp. 219–47. Georgetown University Round Table on Languages and Linguistics 1981. Washington DC: Georgetown University Press.

Labov, William and David Fanshel

1977 *Therapeutic Discourse.* New York: Academic.

Labov, William and Joshua Waletzky

1967 Narrative Analysis: Oral Versions of Personal Experience. In *Essays on the Verbal and Visual Arts,* ed. June Helm, pp. 12–44. Seattle: University of Washington Press for the AES.

Limón, José E.

1983 Legendry, Metafolklore, and Performance: A Mexican-American Example. *Western Folklore* 42:191–208.

Littleton, C. Scott

1965 A Two-Dimensional Scheme for the Classification of Narratives. *Journal of American Folklore* 78:21–7.

Lord, Albert

1953 Homer's Originality: Dictated Texts. *Transactions and Proceedings of the American Philological Association* 84:124–34.

1960 *The Singer of Tales.* Cambridge, MA: Harvard University Press.

McDowell, John H.

1979 *Children's Riddling.* Bloomington: Indiana University Press.

1982 Beyond Iconicity: Ostension in Kamsá Mythic Narrative. *Journal of the Folklore Institute* 19:119–39.

Mills, W.S.

1950 *History of Van Zandt County.* Canton, Texas.

Mink, Louis O.

1978 Narrative Form as a Cognitive Instrument. In *The Writing of History,* ed. Robert H. Canary and Henry Kozicki, pp. 129–49. Madison: University of Wisconsin Press.

1981 Everyman His or Her Own Annalist. In *On Narrative,* ed. W.J.T. Mitchell, pp. 233–9. Chicago: University of Chicago Press.

Morris, Charles

1946 *Signs, Language and Behavior.* New York: Braziller.

Mullen, Patrick B.

1976 The Tall Tale Style of a Texas Raconteur. In *Folk Narrative Research,* ed. Juha Pentikäinen and Tuula Juurikka, pp. 302–11. Helsinki: Finnish Literature Society.

1978 *I Heard the Old Fisherman Say.* Austin: University of Texas Press.

1981 A Traditional Storyteller in Changing Contexts. In *"And Other Neighborly Names,"* ed. Richard Bauman and Roger D. Abrahams, pp. 266–79. Austin: University of Texas Press.

Myerhoff, Barbara

1978 *Number Our Days.* New York: Simon and Schuster.

Nicolaisen, Wilhelm F.H.

1984 The Structure of Narrated Time in the Folktale. In *Le Conte: Pourquoi? Comment?,* pp. 417–36. Paris: Éditions du CNRS.

Ochs, Elinor

1979 Transcription as Theory. In *Developmental Pragmatics,* ed. Elinor Ochs and Bambi Schieffelin, pp. 43–72. New York: Academic.

Ong, Walter

1982 *Orality and Literacy: The Technologizing of the Word.* London and New York: Methuen.

Opland, Jeff

1983 *Xhosa Oral Poetry: Aspects of a Black South African Tradition.* Cambridge: Cambridge University Press.

Paredes, Américo and Richard Bauman, eds.

1972 *Toward New Perspectives in Folklore.* Austin: University of Texas Press.

Philips, Susan U.

1975 *Teasing, Punning, and Putting People On.* Working Papers in Sociolinguistics No. 28. Austin: Southwest Educational Development Laboratory.

Polanyi, Livia

1982 Literary Complexity in Everyday Storytelling. In *Spoken and Written Language,* ed. Deborah Tannen, pp. 155–70. Norwood, NJ: Ablex.

Pratt, Mary Louise

1977 *Toward a Speech Act Theory of Literary Discourse.* Bloomington: Indiana University Press.

Preston, Dennis

1982 'Ritin' Fowklower Daun' Rong: Folklorists' Failures in Phonology. *Journal of American Folklore* 95:304–26.

Rickford, John R.

1976 Riddling and Lying: Participation and Performance. In *A Festschrift for Charles A. Ferguson,* ed. Joshua A. Fishman, pp. 657–75. The Hague: Mouton.

Rimmon-Kenan, Shlomith

1983 *Narrative Fiction: Contemporary Poetics.* London and New York: Methuen.

Roemer, Danielle M.
1977 A Social Interactional Analysis of Anglo Children's Folklore: Catches and Narratives. Doctoral dissertation in Anthropology, University of Texas.

Röhrich, Lutz
1977 *Der Witz*. Stuttgart: Metzler.

Sacks, Harvey
1974 An Analysis of the Course of a Joke's Telling in Conversation. In *Explorations in the Ethnography of Speaking*, ed. Richard Bauman and Joel Sherzer, pp. 337–53. Cambridge: Cambridge University Press.

Sartain, James Alfred
1932 *History of Walker County, Georgia*, vol. 1. Dalton, GA: A.J. Showalter.

Scholes, Robert
1981 Language, Narrative, and Anti-Narrative. In *On Narrative*, ed. W.J.T. Mitchell, pp. 200–8. Chicago: University of Chicago Press.

Schrager, Sam
1983 What Is Social in Oral History? *International Journal of Oral History* 4:76–98.

Schwartzman, Helen B.
1984 Stories at Work: Play in an Organizational Context. In *Text, Play, and Story: The Construction and Reconstruction of Self and Society*, ed. Edward M. Bruner, pp. 80–93. Washington, DC: American Ethnological Society.

Sherzer, Joel
1982a Poetic Structuring of Kuna Discourse: The Line. *Language in Society* 11:371–90.
1982b The Interplay of Structure and Function in Kuna Narrative, or: How to Grab a Snake in the Darien. In *Analyzing Discourse: Text and Talk*, ed. Deborah Tannen, pp. 306–22. Georgetown University Round Table on Languages and Linguistics 1981. Washington, DC: Georgetown University Press.
1985 Puns and Jokes. In *Handbook of Discourse Analysis*, vol. 3 *(Discourse and Dialogue)*, ed. Teun A. Van Dijk, pp. 213–21. London: Academic Press.

Silverstein, Michael
1985 The Culture of Language in Chinookan Narrative Texts; or, On Saying that . . . in Chinook. In *Grammar Inside and Outside the Clause: Some Approaches From the Field*, ed. Johanna Nichols and Anthony Woodbury, pp. 132–74. New York: Cambridge University Press.

Simmel, Georg
1950 *The Sociology of Georg Simmel*, transl. and ed. Kurt Wolff. Glencoe: Free Press.

Sitton, Thad, ed.
1983 *The Loblolly Book*. Austin: Texas Monthly Press.

Smith, Barbara Herrnstein
1968 *Poetic Closure*. Chicago: University of Chicago Press.
1981 Narrative Versions, Narrative Theories. In *On Narrative*, ed. W.J.T. Mitchell, pp. 209–32. Chicago: University of Chicago Press.

Stahl, Sandra

1977a The Oral Personal Narrative in Its Generic Context. *Fabula* 18:18–39.

1977b The Personal Narrative as Folklore. *Journal of the Folklore Institute* 14:9–30.

1983 Personal Experience Stories. In *Handbook of American Folklore*, ed. Richard M. Dorson, pp. 268–75. Bloomington: Indiana University Press.

Sternberg, Meir

1982 Proteus in Quotation-Land: Mimesis and the Forms of Reported Discourse. *Poetics Today* 3(2):107–56.

Stewart, Susan

1982 The Epistemology of the Horror Story. *Journal of American Folklore* 95:33–50.

Stoeltje, Beverly J.

1981 Cowboys and Clowns: Rodeo Specialists and the Ideology of Work and Play. In *"And Other Neighborly Names": Social Process and Cultural Image in Texas Folklore*, ed. Richard Bauman and Roger D. Abrahams, pp. 123–51. Austin: University of Texas Press.

Sydnor, Charles S.

1948 *The Development of Southern Sectionalism, 1819–1848.* Baton Rouge: Louisiana State University Press.

Tallman, Richard

1974 A Generic Approach to the Practical Joke. *Southern Folklore Quarterly* 38:259–74.

1975 Where Stories are Told: A Nova Scotia Storyteller's Milieu. *American Review of Canadian Studies* 5:17–41.

Tannen, Deborah, ed.

1982 *Spoken and Written Language.* Norwood, NJ: Ablex.

1984 *Coherence in Spoken and Written Discourse.* Norwood, NJ: Ablex.

Taylor, Archer

1970 The Anecdote: A Neglected Genre. In *Medieval Literature and Folklore Studies,* ed. Jerome Mandel and Bruce Rosenberg, pp. 223–8. New Brunswick, NJ: Rutgers University Press.

Tedlock, Dennis

1972a On the Translation of Style in Oral Narrative. In *Toward New Perspectives in Folklore,* ed. Américo Paredes and Richard Bauman, pp. 114–33. Austin: University of Texas Press.

1972b Pueblo Literature: Style and Verisimilitude. In *New Perspectives on the Pueblos,* ed. Alfonso Ortiz, pp. 219–42. Albuquerque: University of New Mexico Press.

1983 *The Spoken Word and the Work of Interpretation.* Philadelphia: University of Pennsylvania Press.

Thompson, Stith

1946 *The Folktale.* New York: Dryden.

1955–8 *Motif-Index of Folk Literature.* 6 vols. Bloomington: Indiana University Press.

1961 *The Types of the Folktale,* 2nd rev. ed. Helsinki: Folklore Fellows Communication no. 184.

Toelken, Barre
    1979 *The Dynamics of Folklore*. Boston: Houghton-Mifflin.
Tompkins, Jane P., ed.
    1980 *Reader-Response Criticism*. Baltimore: Johns Hopkins University Press.
Turner, Victor
    1974 *Dramas, Fields, and Metaphors*. Ithaca: Cornell University Press.
Urban, Greg
    1984 Speech about Speech in Speech about Action. *Journal of American Folklore*
        97:310–28.
Verhoeff, Mary
    1911 *The Kentucky Moutains*, vol. 1. Louisville: John P. Morton.
Watson, Jeanne and Robert J. Potter
    1962 An Analytic Unit for the Study of Interaction. *Human Relations* 12:245–
        63.
Welsch, Roger, ed.
    1981 *Mister, You Got Yourself a Horse*. Lincoln: University of Nebraska Press.
White, Hayden
    1973 *Metahistory*. Baltimore: Johns Hopkins University Press.
Woodbury, Anthony
    1985 The Functions of Rhetorical Structure: A Study of Central Alaskan Yupik
        Eskimo Discourse. *Language in Society* 14:153–90.

INDEX

9 780521 311113